Getting Married?

BUILDING YOUR MARRIAGE BEFORE IT BEGINS

Chao Tsuma with
James Tsuma Wanje

Getting Married?

ISBN 13: 978-1-59452-828-6 • ISBN: 1-59452-828-4

Published by Oasis International Ltd.

Oasis International is a ministry devoted to growing discipleship through publishing African voices.

- We ***engage*** Africa's most influential, most relevant, and best communicators for the sake of the gospel.
- We ***cultivate*** local and global partnerships in order to publish and distribute high-quality books and Bibles.
- We ***create*** contextual content that meets the specific needs of Africa, has the power to transform individuals and societies, and gives the church in Africa a global voice.

Oasis is: *Satisfying Africa's Thirst for God's Word*. For more information, go to oasisinternational.com.

Printed in India.

22 23 24 25 26 27 28 29 30 31 BPI 10 9 8 7 6 5 4 3 2 1

Chao and James Wanje have written the guide that I have often longed for in my work as marriage educator. The environment in which young people meet and get married has changed significantly over time. This tool will help them safely navigate towards healthy and sustainable marriages. It includes relatable stories illustrating dilemmas young Africans face, questions to discuss with their partner in a non-threatening way, a gracious and non-judgemental approach, and worksheets that pull the couple to explore their unique backgrounds. I will definitely be recommending this book everywhere I go.

—Modupe Ehirim, Founder and Lead Counsellor at The Right Fit Marriage Academy

As a Kenyan and Canadian who have been married just over 13 years, we could easily relate to many issues covered in this magnificent book. We wish we had had such an excellent resource to prepare us for marriage! We do lots of premarital counselling in our church, which this book will easily complement. We highly recommend this book as a marriage resource for those intending to get married, for the already married seeking to mentor others, and for ministers who serve in such ministries.

—Stanley and Christa Gitonga, Lead pastors at PEFA Runda

Chao and James share from the depth of their relationship with God and the breadth of their over 20 years of experience preparing couples for marriage. Having used materials for non-Africans, they invested time and research to provide a rich, edifying book that connects with the African context. This is a gem for those planning to get married soon, those courting, counsellors, pastors, people keen on enriching their marriages, and everyone passionate about family.

—Rev Benson Kuira Irungu, Senior Pastor of Membley Baptist Church, Ruiru

I like the way James and Chao discussed how we can take the good from our culture and traditions and make it part of our marriages today. It was a breath of fresh air! They relate to the readers by using their own experiences as examples. The fictional story of Jabali and Karembo is right on point. It captures the African audience, who relate to stories. I was really impressed that after each chapter there is an opportunity to act on the information and make commitments.

I can't wait for this material to become available, especially for us who are in marriage ministries. This resource will equip us as we strive to help couples in their relationships.

—Pastor Charles Macharia, Firm Foundation Ministries

Marriage is a powerful witness for Christ and His kingdom. *Getting Married?* celebrates marriage and helps cultivate love and maturity. James and Dr Chao Wanje have been involved in marriage enrichment and reconciliation for over 24 years. Dr Chao enjoys mentoring and Minister James is a devout kingdom man. They have poured into the lives of hundreds of couples throughout Kenya and abroad. This book is a must-read for beginning couples, couples in their golden years of marriage, and for those in between.

—Pastor Ron and Star Nelson, founders of Sowing Seeds of Joy in Dallas, TX

I have had the privilege of mentoring young couples preparing for marriage. Without a shadow of doubt, this is my new go-to tool. Chao and James have done a wonderful job providing a delightful, easy-to-use guide that couples and mentors alike will appreciate.

—Pastor John Paul Mugendi, Senior Pastor of Karen Community Church

Oh, what a wonderful guide these beautiful people have written! They guide the couple to discuss their hopes and their families' expectations, to identify and address red flags, and how to come together to resolve differences. Knowing James and Chao as we have for 20 years, each word has been inspired by their love for Jesus, their love for their people, and their desire for marriage to be experienced as the joyful gift from God that it is.

—Ken and Barbara Benson, married 25 years

Chao and James Tsuma paint vivid, relatable, and practical stories that speak powerfully not just because they are real but because they are based on the living word of God. This is an overflow of their lives and ministry distilled over the years. Whoever takes its advice will build their marriage and family for keeps.

—Joseph and Julia Mwanga, Co-founders of Love In Deed

Written in an African context, this book addresses all the things that often go unspoken, and it fills a niche that is sorely missing. It provides wise counsel from a biblical perspective in a non-judgemental way. Highly, highly recommended. Churches and pastors need to be recommending this to their congregations.

—Matt and Kelly Elmore, Missionaries and International Director of African Christian Outreach

I read this invaluable resource with great joy. Biblical and clearly practical, the built-in interactions help the couple to talk through expectations and issues in a healthy way. I heartily endorse this book. I believe it can help non-African couples as well.

—Dr Howard Ostendorff, S. & E. Africa Coordinator for Freedom In Christ International

Truly a delight to read. This book offers wonderful wisdom on communication, roles, finances, sex, and much more! I especially enjoyed the many real-life examples and couples' stories that were shared in the book. If you're planning to get married, do your marriage a favour and grab a copy of this book. You will not regret it!

—Michael and Muthoni Waiyaki, married nine years

Timely, well-written, and easy to read, this book is also full of deep truths to anchor marriages in God. Having been impacted by the ministry and lives of Chao and James Wanje, I highly recommend this book. It will inspire you to accomplish God's purposes through the institution of marriage and equip you to build a godly legacy.

—Pastor Felix Onyango, author of
The Quest for Greatness* and *Anointed for God's Purpose

Second to the church, marriage is the most beautiful institution our God ever established. However, no one is born knowing how to be or stay married. People need preparation and mentorship. *Getting Married?* is a well-researched and biblically-centred premarital tool. You will enjoy meeting the fictional couple, Jabali and Karembo, who walk alongside you as you prepare for your marriage. Pastors and counsellors, you need to grab this masterpiece! It will make your work easy and most definitely enjoyable.

—Pastor Isaac and Rayhab Macharia,
Lead Pastors of Trinity Chapel Kampala

This study guide is for anyone preparing to be married, as well as those who skipped this stage – anyone concerned about building a lasting marriage that will be a legacy for generations to come. We enjoyed seeing the different scenarios in each chapter, showing what different characters went through before and even after marriage. James and Dr Chao Tsuma often shared their experiences, which makes any reader feel like marriage is not a mistake but God's way to show his excellence.

—Grace and Eric Kavivya, married nine years

Getting Married?

1

Getting the Most out of "Getting Married?"

Zippy and Yohana

Zippy was in medical school and Yohana was finishing his accounting programme. They had known each other since they were young, but they did not start dating until they went to college. As she prepared to finish her internship and as he entered the workforce, he asked her to marry him. Their friends were overjoyed to hear the news. They also encouraged the couple to reach out to us to help them prepare for marriage.

Soon they were meeting in our home. She would ride on public transport for about two hours, and he would meet her at the stage that took them to our house.

We learned that she is the oldest in her family and was raised by a single mother. As soon as she went into high school, she found odd jobs. Every single shilling she earned she shared with her mother. Together they were able to educate and feed the family. She said, "My mother is so used to me taking care of everyone, including her. As I prepare for marriage, I am afraid that she is expecting me to continue taking care of them. She does not see that I will now have my own home and a husband, and we will need to make financial decisions together."

Yohana was concerned about their pastor's expectations. "Our pastor has always known that he can count on us. He is used to calling me any time, day or night, to attend to church emergencies. When I told him we were getting married, he said he was happy that we both were from the same church, and together we could do more for the church. I am not sure how I will help him realize that I now have a family, and I cannot be as involved as I was when I was single."

Zippy also shared, "I was sexually active before we started dating. While we have chosen not to engage in sex until we get married, I am still concerned that my past choices could affect sex in our marriage. I am hoping that both of us can work through any areas of fear, anxiety, or unforgiveness."

Every Friday for three months, they arrived at our home, ready to learn, share, and discuss. We talked about finances, sex, and how to manage the expectations of others. They were vulnerable with each other and with us. We watched this couple go from being unsure of themselves to preparing their parents, the church, and other people close to them to expect things to be different as they moved into otheir marriage.

The day of the wedding came. They exchanged their vows and went on to build their home. Later Zippy told us, "We still have to explain to my mother that she cannot fully depend on us for her financial upkeep. But since we talked about this during our sessions on preparing for marriage, we are not only in agreement about how to continue to work with my mother, we are also careful that we do not allow her to come between us."

Yohana said, "We cannot begin to imagine how we would have started off our marriage had we not chosen to take the time to prepare."

Rehema and Patrick

Rehema's father received word that he should be expecting guests at his home. Knowing how important this visit was, he invited the village elders, some of whom were his relatives, to host the guests after their eight-hour journey. The women cleaned, cooked, and sang as they prepared for the occasion. Today, two men from two different communities were about to meet for the first time. Their children had fallen in love. Rehema and Patrick were seeking their parents' blessings to marry. Today, the two men would agree that they were happy their children had made the decision to build a home together.

Coming from eight hours away, Patrick's father was also accompanied by elders from his village and women who carried gifts to give to the family. The visit brought a sense of excitement to the village. Dowry negotiations were finalized, handshakes were plentiful, and the two families celebrated coming together.

This couple enjoyed a pre-wedding party with friends, a bridal shower, the wedding rehearsal, and before they knew it, they exchanged their vows. Off they went to live happily ever after!

They returned to their new home from their honeymoon and settled back into a regular routine. Soon *happily ever after* began to feel like *sadly ever after*. It quickly dawned on them that it was one thing to dance at their wedding, and another thing to balance the books at the end of the month.

Patrick said, "We were both employed and were earning a generous income. Neither of us is careless with money. We just could not figure out how to best agree and spend money in our marriage."

Rehema said, "With the different financial expectations from our extended families, the need for us to give towards church and community needs, and also our desire to save up for our home, we felt overwhelmed by the responsibilities. It did not take long before the money become a lot shorter than the month."

It was one thing to exchange vows before a room of witnesses – "to love, honour, and cherish; for richer, for poorer; in sickness and in health" – and it was another thing to live out those vows.

Rehema said, "When we agreed to start having children, he said that in his culture all the children were named after their father's family. I could not believe what I was hearing. All along, I had assumed we would agree on how to name our children. To him, this was not up for discussion. You can only imagine the hurt I felt."

Patrick said, "I thought I was being a leader in our home by making decisions, including how to name our children. The more I tried to lead, the more I felt her resistance. I felt frustrated. I wanted my wife to be happy that I was responsible for my family. Instead, she grew more and more distant from me."

When we met them, Rehema told us, "We were feeling a strain in our marriage. I am convinced, had we taken the time to prepare ourselves for our marriage, we would have known how to better confront the different challenges we faced."

Both couples loved each other, celebrated their weddings, and moved on to start building their marriages. But only one couple took the time to prepare. They built a foundation that made them more intentional in growing together as husband and wife. When faced with challenges, their foundation was already solid. The other couple did not prepare, so it took them time after they were married to learn how to best grow together. They wished they had talked through their backgrounds and expectations beforehand, rather than being surprised when issues came up with the full force of emotion.

Why Preparing for Marriage Is Important

You might have some hesitations or concerns about preparing for marriage. Let's address them by explaining why preparing for marriage is important.

Preparing for marriage is worth the time and money you invest in the process. You will find the time and money for what is important. When we were young and visited my grandparents for the holidays, Grandmother would make sure to prepare a special meal of *chapati* and beans for us. Grandmother could have easily said there was no time to cook the beans on a three-stone *jiko* stove or roll out the *chapati* dough and fry each one. She could have said it was too expensive to buy the ingredients needed to make the *chapati*, which were a luxury compared to the cost of her everyday food. She could have said she couldn't possibly do all the cleaning and preparation by herself.

Instead, she focused on the joy she would see on our faces once we found out we were having *chapati* and beans, the sweet fellowship around the fire in the kitchen, and the excitement of us coming back for a repeat of this same treat. Because we were important to her, Grandmother was always willing to spend time and money to make us happy. We were worth it to her. When you prepare for your marriage, you prioritize your marriage over other things that could take your time. You communicate that marriage is worth investing in by making the time and finding the money to prepare for it.

Marriage is a covenant between the two of you and God. It is a commitment you will make, not only in the presence of witnesses, but also with God at the centre. Your marriage has the potential to make the invisible God visible. God's attributes can potentially be seen in your marriage as you choose to love each other, forgive one another, be patient with one another, and be faithful in keeping your vows. Marriage is the metaphor God uses to describe Christ's beautiful love for the church. If you are going to make such a powerful covenant, you can and should make the time to prepare for it.

Preparing for marriage also helps you transition into another season of your life. Marriage is a rite of passage. After you exchange your vows, things will never be the way they were before. You are transitioning from being single to being married. You are moving from your childhood home and adding another community into your relationships. Don't be in a hurry to say, "I do." As a Swahili proverb says, *Haraka haraka haina baraka*, which means, "Hurrying has no blessings." Take time to prepare for this lifetime commitment to love. It's worth it because marriage is a celebration, a joy, and a love relationship like Christ loves the church.

All marriages face challenges. But why go through the pain of trial-and-error when you could be equipped with skills to face them? By preparing for marriage, you can reap the benefits and joy sooner. Preparing for marriage helps you to talk openly about personal issues, especially issues that we are not culturally accustomed to talking openly about, such as sex. As you learn about each other's backgrounds, you will come to understand better where the other person is coming from and reduce your frustrations.

Preparing for your marriage, not just your wedding, helps you see some of the blind spots you might be ignoring. If there is a time when you need to ask yourselves the hard questions, process through any issues you might have, and seek help if need be, it is before you get married. An engaged couple had already picked a wedding date when we encouraged them to take time off and work on their personal issues. He had confessed to her his need for help to overcome his addiction to pornography. She admitted she needed help to learn how to work through her anger issues. We referred them to professional counsellors who saw them on a regular basis. It took them another six months to work on those issues before they were ready for their wedding. They realized that once you say, "I do", it becomes more complicated to change that decision! Now is the time to evaluate whether or not you are ready for this lifelong journey.

Our Story

We know how important preparing for marriage is because we experienced what it is like to begin a marriage without preparation. We don't recommend it!

We had learned well how to plan for a wedding, and where we needed help, we turned to our friends and family. But we did not know how anyone planned for a marriage, and we did not try to find out how other couples planned for their marriages. Individually we had our understandings of what it meant to be in a marriage, but we had not taken the time to discuss and agree how to work together to grow our marriage. And so, during the times of conflict, instead of fighting for our marriage together, we fought against each other and also assumed something was wrong with our marriage. Instead of involving each other in our individual interests and goals, we tried to protect those interests from each other. Slowly, we began to notice that we were drifting apart from each other. To anyone around us, we looked healthy and happy, but in private we felt isolated and trapped.

For five years, we knew there was more to marriage than what we were experiencing, but we didn't know how to find it. We knew that marriage was meant to be enjoyed and not endured. We were enduring our way through our union. Then a mentor couple invited us to join other couples who were meeting to build their marriages. We feared it was too late for us, but with the help of this mentor couple, we started our pre-marriage preparation after we were married. We discussed expectations, learned how to best resolve conflicts, how to work as a team, how to handle different pressures in marriage, and more. With every lesson, our relationship improved. Soon we were recommending these discussions to other couples. We also made a commitment to encourage every couple we knew who was preparing for their wedding to take the time to prepare for their marriage. This started our journey to help couples prepare for their marriages – which we have been doing now for more than 20 years.

Stories That Speak to Your Heart

For the first 15 years of preparing couples for their marriages, we primarily used material written for a non-African audience. While the principles are timeless, we had to adapt the material to fit each couple's cultural contexts. We were convinced that when we spoke to the couple's context, they more fully understood, appreciated, and experienced its content. I (Chao) eventually researched how to make premarital counselling more relevant to African contexts for my PhD.

Five years ago, we started using my research insights in our work with couples. Our discussions quickly became more lively and relatable. For example, when we talked about finances, we included how to plan to support other family members, give towards community needs, and help those in need of medical and funeral funds. Couples lit up when we raised the issue of how to choose to name their children. One couple wanted to know, "What does the Bible say about us choosing not to name our children after our own parents?" In our cultures, we tend to shy away from talking about sex, and even when it is taught, the different genders do not learn together. But God is not embarrassed to talk about sex, and we should not be embarrassed either.

Our approach was working so well that we decided we needed to write our own premarital preparation guide. Other mentor couples had begun requesting material that speaks to our language, to our culture, and to our understanding. They wanted concepts they could easily transfer to the couples they mentored. In this book, you will keep your African lenses on as you discuss topics such as gender roles and responsibilities, relating with in-laws, resolving conflicts, sexual intimacy, and working as a team with your finances. You will be challenged to consider how you should preserve some traditional views on marriage, modify some of them to fit with biblical beliefs, and do away with those that contrast with biblical beliefs about marriage. This book provides you with truths that will draw you closer to God as you also grow closer to each other. You will be equipped to prepare for a godly African marriage!

Our people grew up with learning lessons by listening to stories. We affirm African ways of learning by ensuring this book is full of stories to help in illustration and application. We use relatable examples of real couples we have worked with from different tribes. You will also have the opportunity to hear our story as a couple. We will give you both our professional experience and our married life experience. Finally, we also included a fictional couple, Jabali and Karembo, who will walk alongside you in the journey of preparing for marriage. Let's introduce them to you.

Jabali and Karembo

Karembo's forehead was sweating and her hair was starting to itch. She and nine other girls had been sitting in one position for about an hour, draped in fabric that covered their faces and bodies from head to toe. A tent shielded them from the sun, but also added more heat to an already hot day. Her friends whispered and giggled, loving every moment of it. They were the decoys used to trick Jabali into picking the wrong girl.

She had played their part twice before at her two closest friends' traditional ceremonies, but she wasn't feeling quite so giggly now that she was the focus of attention. Her relatives and Jabali's relatives had gathered from far and wide for this event. She sat quietly with her hands clasped.

Karembo saw Jabali's feet from underneath her veil. He was getting closer. *Does he know me well enough to recognize me?*

They had known each other since they were in university. Jabali was the guy with a big heart whom everyone knew they could count on. Karembo was the beautiful, wise, focused, and hard-working girl who was admired by her peers. He was two years ahead of her in university, and they met a few months before he graduated. The first thing she noticed about him, besides his strong frame, were his dimples.

After he graduated, Jabali moved to the city where both their parents lived and found employment. Every weekend, he made the four-hour trip to go and see her in university. It surprised no one when, a few months after she graduated, he asked her to marry him.

Jabali wasn't worried about identifying Karembo. To him, she had always stood out from the crowd. The crowd cheered to distract him. He stayed focused, whistling softly as he inspected the covered girls, one after another. He wasn't allowed to touch or talk to them to make his decision. But Karembo and her friends had given him hints before the ceremony started.

"This one is my bride!" he said.

The crowd shouted with jubilation. Jabali's aunties and cousins hugged Karembo and carried her in the air. They quickly removed the covers she had on to show her off to the crowd. Jabali's uncles and male cousins formed a circle around him and made a warlike cry, sending tremors of excitement throughout the village. Somebody came with a drum. People started dancing to the beat. It was a bit more boisterous than usual for Karembo's family, but soon they were pulled into the dance circle too.

As the traditional ceremony drew to a close, Jabali and Karembo sighed with relief, although they still had much ahead of them. We can't wait for you to follow Jabali and Karembo as they journey through preparing for their marriage!

More Companions on the Journey

In addition to Jabali and Karembo and us, James and Chao, we encourage you to find some real-life companions for your journey. As a proverb reminds us, "If you want to go fast, walk alone. If you want to walk far, walk together."

Some people find it invasive to sit one-on-one with a pastor, church leader, or a stranger and share about their lives. On the other hand, some couples who go through group counselling classes wish there were a forum for them to ask personal questions. This book provides you with a winning alternative. You could work through the book just the two of you, but we recommend finding a mentor couple to guide you in the process of reading this book. Your experience will not only transform you and your future marriage, it will also transform the mentor couple's marriage. Choose someone you feel comfortable talking to. You will have a forum where you can open up about your joys and struggles and hear about theirs. You will have a couple to support you in prayer and give insight as they observe your relationship. The mentor couple will not only be there for you before you get married, but even after the wedding, they may become long-term friends and advisors.

Who might you identify as a good potential mentor couple? They do not have to hold powerful positions in the community, though they can. They could be your pastor, Bible study leaders, or a couple you've asked to be in your wedding party. We recommend finding a couple who has been married for at least five years and is willing to share their own successes and failures. Think of a couple whose marriage you want to emulate, a couple with whom you both feel comfortable.

How to Use This Book

We begin the book by laying the foundation of understanding what marriage is. We discuss cultural and biblical reasons why people get married, the expectations we carry from our cultures and backgrounds, and some basic biblical principles for marriage. Then we build on that foundation by tackling specific topics that commonly affect marriages, such as communication, roles, finances, sex, and in-laws. At the end, we return to the foundation with a reminder of the importance of depending on God in your marriage.

If you choose to use this book by meeting just the two of you, then agree to meet weekly or once every other week. Since it is just the two of you, you will be able to pace yourselves, take the time you need to discuss the different topics, and seek answers to questions that come up along the way. Agree on the time and place to meet. We recommend that you begin with the end in mind, making a plan to finish the lessons at least four weeks before your wedding day.

If you choose to ask a mentor couple to guide you in the process, which is what we highly recommend, agree with them on the day of the week, the time, and place to meet. You can agree to meet once a week or once every other week. Meeting with both a husband and wife will provide insight from both the male and female perspectives. This couple will not only be investing in your marriage, they will also be investing in their marriage as well. We recommend that they get their own copy of this book (or you could gift it to them!). They can start by reading the section on pages 192-196 called **For the Mentor Couple**.

Conclusion

After throwing the bouquet, we want you to know you do not have to throw in the towel! We will do our best to ensure that after you have danced your way late into the night on your wedding, you will be equipped to go on to build a healthy home. We will walk you through the tried-and-true principles that have built many marriages, including our own marriage of more than 20 years. We hope someday you will also mentor younger couples who come after you.

Digging Deeper

The "Digging Deeper" section at the end of each chapter gives you the opportunity to apply what you have learned and immediately put it into practice.

Individual Reflection

This section will have questions for you to reflect on individually.

For this session, before you move onto the next chapter, find the **Personal History Data** sheet in the Activities and Resources section on pages 176-182. This section is to help you understand your past, share it with your intended other, and begin to see how your past can influence your future marriage.

Discussion

Then you will come together for a discussion.

If you are working through the manual just the two of you, make the time to discuss your answers to the questions on your **Personal History Data**.

Prayer

Each chapter encourages you to wrap up by praying together.

Pray together for God to bless your preparation for marriage and to guide you in approaching a mentor couple.

Mentors

This portion gives advice on how to talk through the content with your mentors when you meet with them.

Be prepared to share some insights from your **Personal History Data** with your mentor couple during your first meeting.

Take It Further

You will also notice ideas to take it further. Here we will give you opportunities to do fun activities together, connect with other people, and enjoy each other.

Approach a mentor couple to go through this book with you. They could be someone from your church, your family, or your community who are strong believers and have been married for at least five years. You'll be so glad you did!

2

Expectations

Jabali and Karembo had just returned from the village where they held their traditional wedding. It was six months before their church wedding, and they were beginning to run errands to prepare. Jabali was dropping Karembo off one evening. He stopped the car and got out to open her door, but she had already taken off to her house. She raced through her parents' living room. Her favourite aunt sat at the coffee table visiting with her parents, but she almost forgot to greet them before excusing herself. She closed the door of the bedroom she shared with her sisters and flopped onto the bed.

No, she and Jabali had not quarrelled. Yes, she loved him dearly and she could not wait to be married to him. It was just that she was upset and confused by things she had noticed that night.

She had overheard him on the phone with his parents making arrangements for the upcoming holidays: "Sure, mum, Karembo and I are planning to be there. Oh, don't worry about the two goats, I will buy those." Jabali's family was welcoming and easy to interact with, but it was feeling more and more like he expected them to go to his village every holiday. She had also seen how Jabali dished out money like a stereotypical politician every time they were around relatives. She was happy that he was generous, but she worried that he didn't plan how much money he would give out.

Then, before he dropped her off, they had stopped by his aunt's house. While Jabali visited with his uncle, his aunt chatted with Karembo. "I just feel I am adding another daughter into my family. Bless the Lord!" the aunt beamed. "I hope you have more than one son, that way you can name the first after Jabali's dad and the second after my husband."

Karembo did not respond. She wondered, *So, they expect us to name all our children after their family. What if I want to name a child after my father? Some of my friends chose not to name their children the traditional way and instead gave them names of their own choices. Why can't we?*

Over dinner, she had noticed that Jabali seemed comfortable waiting for her to pray before they ate. He had mentioned how he enjoyed listening to her pray and to what she was learning in her study of the Bible, but it bothered her that she took more initiative than him on spiritual matters.

Karembo worried: *What am I getting myself into? What if we get married and nothing changes? I don't know how I could bring this up with Jabali. Why didn't anyone tell me how much there is to think about as you go into marriage? Her sister's poster of a movie star couple caught her eye. They were embracing and staring into each other's eyes. She felt they were mocking her. Is this supposed to happen in love stories?*

Meanwhile, Jabali was surprised that Karembo hadn't even said goodbye before dashing into the house! As he started the car, he thought about how ever since he met Karembo, life had not been the same for him. He could not wait for her to be his wife. He envisioned a life of peace, teamwork, and laughter. But now something was the matter, and he couldn't put his finger on it. He suspected that Karembo was hiding something from him.

Jabali found himself in a difficult place: if he confronted Karembo, he could make matters worse. If he kept quiet, the drift he noticed between them could get worse. What was he to do?

Discuss Your Expectations

Like Karembo, everyone beginning marriage has expectations. Like Jabali, many people are reluctant to bring up uncomfortable conversations. As a result, they begin their marriages in the dark, never having discussed their expectations. Some people fear that bringing up concerns will make it seem as if they do not care enough for the other person. Some may have uneasy feelings but may have grown up in a home where uncomfortable topics were not discussed. Others hope that once they are married, the issues will either sort themselves out or come up naturally.

The best place to begin to discuss expectations is before you say "I do". Walking into marriage without realistic expectations can affect the health of your marriage. You can choose to address these concerns before they become big conflicts. This can protect your relationship and set a precedent for how you will confront issues when you get married. Discussing expectations before marriage also helps you to make a smoother transition, begin to build a strong foundation, and determine your compatibility in marriage.

Our Story

When James and I (Chao) first got married, I purchased a beautiful picnic basket for romantic picnics in the park on Sunday afternoons, just the two of us. One day, I wanted to surprise James and show him what an organized wife he had married! James was one of the church leaders and he usually left church after everyone had left. But I asked him to please leave his Sunday afternoon open for us to go and spend some quiet time at the park.

I left James at church and quickly got ready at home. I waited and waited … Finally, James came home, but it was already night. I opened the door and, without saying a word to him, went straight to bed.

This was the first of several occasions when our beautiful picnic basket would go unopened and unused. James would apologize and promise that next time he would ask someone else to help at church so that he could come home early.

The same trend happened in other scenarios. I expected James to make me his number one human priority. When he did not pick me up on time, I interpreted it as him loving me less. When I fussed about him coming home late and not letting me know in advance, he interpreted it as my lack of concern for what he valued. James expected me to understand that he had hobbies that would take him away from me for longer than expected. In the process, we both hurt each other.

It was not until we were married that we finally gathered the courage to have an open conversation about expectations. Don't put it off as we did! Had we discussed expectations before we got married, it would have given us a foundation from which to start communicating. It would have also alleviated some of the stresses of feeling misunderstood, ignored, and unloved. It would also have given us tools to use when we had differing expectations in our marriage.

The next Saturday, Karembo and Jabali were scheduled to meet with two potential caterers. At the meeting with the first caterer, Jabali noticed that Karembo went through the motions. She said all the right things and contributed to the conversation, but the glow on her face had dimmed. Jabali felt frustrated. It didn't seem like Karembo was just being moody. What was it?

Jabali suggested that they grab some lunch before meeting the other caterer. He knew exactly where to take Karembo. She had developed a love for traditional foods. She was not one to suggest eating at a fast food restaurant – except that she had a sweet tooth! After eating at this particular restaurant, he could walk her over to get a scoop of her favourite pistachio ice cream with a touch of coconut.

As they waited for their food, Jabali said, "When I dropped you at your house, you looked upset. Today you seem distracted. What's bothering you?"

Karembo shared about the phone call and the planned visit to his village. She expressed her fears that they would always go to his village for holidays.

Jabali had heard nightmare stories of married women who did not want to visit their in-laws in the villages. For vacation, they wanted to either get away from family, or stay in the city and not entertain much because they wanted their "me time". "But Karembo, I thought you loved my family! It's meant so much to me that you join me every time I visit my family."

She said, "Of course I love your family. It's not that at all. But I want to build our own family too. When will we get to explore places and build memories just for us? How are we going to build our own culture if we keep all the traditions you grew up with?"

"My family has always gone to the village for Christmas. Maybe I assumed that was what we would do too. It never crossed my mind that I could start a new tradition, but it could be fun. Maybe I'll have to think about that some more."

Encouraged, Karembo also brought up her concerns about his freedom with giving. "It is good to be generous, but I'm worried you don't plan how much you will give. When we get married, we will need a budget and savings."

"I guess I haven't paid much attention to saving. I know how to earn income and spend it. But you're good at keeping track of finances. Maybe you could help me."

"There's one more thing that was bothering me. It seems like I'm always the one initiating prayer. I want you to be a spiritual leader."

"What do you mean, a spiritual leader?"

"You know, that's what a husband is supposed to do, just like my dad who led prayers with my mum as I was growing up."

"Am I in a competition with your father?" The words came out of Jabali's mouth before he had time to think. Still, he felt justified in his anger. What if he turned around and told Karembo how he was afraid she would not keep house like he saw his mum keep their home? Would that be fair to her?

Karembo began to cry. Jabali felt an inner brokenness. "I didn't mean it like that, Karembo."

"I'm scared, Jabali."

Their lunch had come, but they hardly touched it. She looked at the clock. They had 10 minutes to cross to the other side of town. There was no way they were going to make it on time.

"Look," Jabali said. "We clearly have some things we need to talk about. But it's a lot for one day. Let's just keep talking."

She nodded and took a deep breath. "Okay." It had been intense, but part of her felt relieved that she had opened up. At least her anxieties were in the open now. And she realized he had a point too. They both had made assumptions, but they were on their way to working through them together.

How to Approach a Conversation about Expectations

Your attitude will influence your conversations about expectations. Romans 12:10 reminds us of the attitude we should have towards each other: "Be devoted to one another in love. Honour one another above yourselves." Even when we sense that things are not going well between us, it is important to honour and love each other. In Ephesians 4:29, Paul gives us guidelines for how to have uncomfortable conversations: "Do not let unwholesome [foul, profane, worthless, vulgar] words ever come out of your mouth, but only such *speech* as is good for building up others, according to the need *and* the occasion, so that it will be a blessing to those who hear [you speak]" (AMP). In Jabali and Karembo's case, they expressed themselves honestly without blaming the other person and listened to each other. Unfortunately, Jabali let something harmful out of his mouth, but he was quick to recognize the mistake and try to repair the damage.

Where We Learn about Expectations

As you discuss your concerns, it helps to identify where you learned these expectations. Our backgrounds often play a big role in what we expect in a relationship. You grew up in two different homes. You are two different people. It makes sense that your preferences, expectations, and future plans may be different. James and I (Chao) found we had made many assumptions about how we would treat each other in marriage based on our backgrounds. We thought that we were both reading from the same script! The only way to begin to understand and work through those differences is by verbally expressing them.

Let's explore how we learn about expectations, using Jabali and Karembo as an example. While we cannot give a list of every place one could learn about expectations, here are four key areas:

1. During courtship. Sometimes we set patterns in dating that we don't expect to continue into marriage, but the other person can be surprised at a change in behaviour.

   Jabali used to take Karembo to his village during their courtship. She did not seem to complain, so he expected this to continue after they got married. Karembo, however, was taking the opportunity to build a relationship with his family before marrying into it, but she hoped they wouldn't travel there every holiday going forward.

2. Our families of origin. From our childhood homes, we learn what it means to relate to others and to be in a family. Our parents' marriage often becomes the default standard in our mind, whether we desire to emulate them or to avoid being like them.

   Karembo's father led devotions in their home, so she expected Jabali to do the same.

3. Culture and traditions. Our cultures, families, and communities have expectations about marriage and the roles of husband and wife. Even though our cultures are changing, these expectations still affect how we relate.

   Jabali assumed his wife would visit his family during the holidays, because in their culture people visited their paternal homes more than their maternal homes. Jabali's aunt assumed they would name their children after Jabali's family, according to his cultural tradition. Even though Karembo resented these arrangements, she felt obligated by culture to keep up appearances and make a good impression on his family. Deep inside, she wished things could be different.

4. The media and outside cultural influences. Our societies are increasingly exposed to other cultures and ideas of marriage. Young people are exposed to different ways of thinking and doing things through an education away from home, peers, movies, books, and music videos. While the intermingling of cultures can be a beautiful thing, couples need to carefully choose what to incorporate from outside and what to keep from the cultures they were influenced by growing up. All these models must be evaluated against Christian standards as well.

    Karembo had seen her friends name their children differently than their parents' generation. She hoped she and Jabali could build their own culture. Additionally, the romance stories Karembo saw in the media made everything look easy, so when she noticed these concerns, she worried something was wrong with her relationship.

Reflecting on where your expectations came from can help you to realize why these expectations are important and how they might be able to change in your new life together.

Reflecting on Your Expectations

After you identify the sources of your expectations, what do you do next? Over the years of working with couples preparing for marriage, Chao and I (James) have found it helps to reflect on why these expectations matter, what lies under them, and what would satisfy the conflict of your expectations. Ask yourself some questions like these:

- Is this a personal conviction, or something I hope for because others expect it of me?

  For example, Jabali should ask himself if he wants to grow as a spiritual leader or if he is pursuing it just because Karembo expects it of him.

- Why did my parents or my culture do things that way?

  Why did Jabali's family expect their children to be named after their family members?

- Are there important underlying values I could preserve, but implement them in a different way?

  Could Jabali and Karembo agree that they value their extended families and agree how regularly or at what season to visit them?

- Is this expectation realistic to expect of the other person?

  Is it realistic for Karembo to expect her new husband to display the same spiritual maturity and leadership as her father?

- Why is this important to me? Why is this important to my intended?

  Why is it important for Karembo to see Jabali be more careful with spending?

- What fears and needs does this expectation bring up in me? In the other person?

  Jabali hears that Karembo is looking for a man who fits her father's profile. He is afraid he will disappoint her.

- How can we still meet each other's expectations, even if we change what we decide to do?

  How could Jabali support people in the village while also setting aside some savings?

- What values do we agree on, even if we have different ways of expressing them?

  Both Jabali and Karembo appear to value generosity, family, and spiritual growth, although they express these differently.

Adjusting Your Expectations

Sometimes we expect the other person to know how to meet our expectations immediately after our wedding day. When discussing our expectations, we need to ask whether this expectation is core to us. If the person did not change, would it be a deal-breaker? Or are we willing to give room for growth?

After what felt like years of frustrations, I, Chao, realized it was unrealistic of me to expect James to be involved in any elaborate plans on a Sunday afternoon. As long as he was in church leadership, I needed to learn to look at Sunday as his work day. I needed to find a day and time when James could be a lot more flexible. Personal reflection helped me evaluate my expectations, improved our relationship, and freed us to find other ways to build our relationship.

It is important to be flexible with the specific hopes we have for how the other person will act or what our marriage will look like. Sometimes our expectations are simply unrealistic, and we need to let them go. Other times, one or both of you may be willing to adjust, but the change may not happen as quickly or smoothly as you hope.

The question to ask then becomes not whether your partner already meets all your expectations, but whether you are willing to learn, grow together, and forgive each other for falling short along the way. Having a teachable spirit is one of the ways to work through expectations. Proverbs 13:18 says: "Whoever disregards discipline comes to poverty and shame, but whoever heeds correction is honoured." Having a teachable spirit brings good results. The other person likes and trusts you more. You become wiser. As Jabali learns the balance between generosity and financial planning, he will continue to grow in wisdom. As you grow in discipline and cultivate a teachable spirit, you will also have fewer conflicts, because you will have learned that meeting each other's expectations is a journey that takes time and patience.

Jabali and Karembo were late to their second meeting but thankfully, their host was able to wait for them. Karembo was more present than she had been in the morning. They decided they preferred the first caterer and headed home. As Jabali dropped Karembo off, he said, "I want to continue the conversation we started today. But I might make a mess of it if we try to do it on our own!"

Karembo said, "What if we asked Krispian and Mishi if we could visit with them?" They both knew and respected this couple from church. The couple had been married for about seven years now. Jabali agreed. With another couple's feedback, hopefully they could work through areas of expectations.

Karembo walked into the kitchen and smiled as she greeted her parents. Her mum was cutting vegetables for dinner and her dad was sipping a cup of tea as he read the newspaper. She poured herself a cup of tea before joining in the dinner preparation. It was going to be okay after all.

Conclusion

It is important that you discuss expectations before you say, "I do." Look under the surface to find out where you learned these expectations and why they are important to you. When you discuss these questions, you will begin to see a pattern form of what you expect in your marriage. You could surprise yourself by making different decisions once you have listened to the other person. In the process, you have the opportunity to know both yourself and the other person better. While you may not discuss every expectation before you get married, you will have a good foundation. You will have addressed what you currently know and will be better equipped to handle expectations going forward.

Starting the conversation now will help you to have a smoother transition, begin to build a strong foundation, and determine your compatibility in marriage.

Dowry!

It is not unusual for some couples preparing for marriage to feel discomfort or even dread at the mention of the word *dowry*. Dowry negotiations are sometimes a source of conflict, not only between the two families, but also between the couple preparing for marriage.

Some people in our cultures cherish the practice and see how it helps unify the two families. Other people see it as an avenue for exploitation, especially for material gain!

It is important to discuss your expectations around this practice together so that you can be prepared and work as a team. Here are some questions to talk through:

- What is your attitude towards dowry?
- What is your family's attitude towards dowry?
- How do you agree or disagree in your attitudes towards dowry?
- If her family asks for dowry, how should you each support the other person?

If you anticipate a negotiation process, commit to praying for it. Trust God to guide the two of you as you stand together in the process. Pray for all the people involved in the process of negotiation.

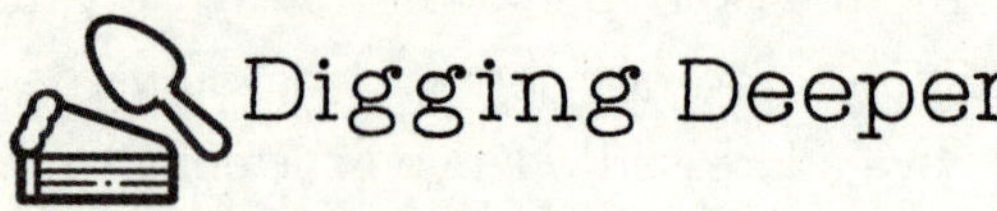

Digging Deeper

Individual Reflection

Find a quiet place with some privacy to complete this section. The aim of this activity is to help you begin to uncover and then discuss expectations before your marriage.

We will address expectations throughout the book. To get comfortable having these conversations, begin with a few simple topics. Answer the following:

1. How do you like to spend your weekend? What hobbies will you pursue individually and as a couple?
2. How often will you entertain guests in your home?
3. Once you get married, how will you decide where to spend your holidays?
4. Where do you plan to live after your wedding?
5. How would you like to spend your honeymoon?

Discussion

Meet together and complete this section. Make sure you choose a place where you can talk uninterrupted.

Take turns sharing your answers to questions 1 to 5. Highlight an area where you seem to agree and an area where you seem to disagree. Use the questions above as a guide to begin talking through areas that seem contentious.

Be prepared to share with your mentor couple an area of agreement and an area of disagreement.

Prayer

Pray together, giving thanks for the areas you agree on and inviting the Holy Spirit to help you in the areas you do not agree on yet.

Mentors

Share with your mentor couple an area of agreement and an area of disagreement.

How did you choose to move forward in the area you disagreed? Are there any expectations you would like to discuss with them?

Take It Further

Visit a place that is important to the other person.

During the visit, ask the other person to share the significance of the place to her or him and any past memories about the place.

3

Why Are You Getting Married?

Karembo called and asked Krispian and Mishi if she and Jabali could visit with them. She remembered them from a few interactions at church, and they quickly set a date to meet.

On the agreed upon day, Jabali and Karembo set out. Never visit a home empty-handed, Karembo's mum had always told her. They made a quick stop at the supermarket and bought some groceries to carry to the couple's home.

"How should we start the conversation?" Karembo asked. She liked to plan ahead, especially since they did not know the couple well.

Jabali said, "It will just happen. We will think as we go." Once again, Karembo remembered how different they were! But sometimes differences complement each other, right?

They hoped to ask Krispian and Mishi to mentor them as they prepared for marriage. "What if they say no?" Karembo asked.

"We cannot know until we ask, right? And even if they say no, they might suggest other couples they know. Either way, it is a win."

Karembo bit her tongue. *It is not the end of the world, Karembo! Just relax.*

Every young couple they knew spoke highly of Krispian and Mishi. They were involved together in a ministry at church, and they were easy to talk to. Mishi seemed calm and did not talk much. She was a magnet to the young ladies at church. Her outgoing husband, Krispian, was easy to spot as he interacted with different personalities at church functions. There was something about Krispian and Mishi's marriage that set them apart from many other couples in the church. "They are perfect for each other," some would say.

As they knocked on the door, Jabali wondered to himself, *I wonder if I finally get to find out what it is about them that seems so unique.* Karembo stood with a grocery bag in one hand, and the other hand lightly touching Jabali's back. She had finally come up with a question to ask. *I would really like to know why they chose to get married in the first place. How did she know he was the one?*

Their hosts opened the door and welcomed them into their home.

You have probably heard your friends, relatives, or other people give reasons why they got married or why they would like to get married. Maybe you are like James and myself (Chao). You have some ideas but have not actively thought through why you are getting married. For you and your intended other, it will help you to appreciate the importance of marriage and prepare yourself if you understand why you are deciding to get married – and why you are choosing to marry each other specifically.

Common Cultural Reasons for Getting Married

As Christians, we date the institution of marriage back to the Garden of Eden when God fashioned Eve for Adam and brought her to him (Genesis 2:21-22). Since that beginning, world communities have celebrated marriages generation after generation. While marriage continues, the reasons why people get married have changed somewhat over time, even since the time our grandparents married.

Marriage is an important rite of passage. Traditionally, this was when a man transitioned from being a "boy" to being considered a man. He was deemed of age to make decisions, not just for himself, but also for the home he was establishing and for the good of the community. Marriage gave both the man and the woman added status in the community. It was the context for having children, and children provided security to the family. Since most of our communities follow a patriarchal set-up, the male children carried the family name forward. Children also provided food security because they helped to till the land and harvest its produce. When girls married, they increased the financial security of their parents' homes because the groom and his family paid dowry. Marriage forged friendships and political alliances, including fostering peace between warring communities.

Some of these reasons from our grandparents' generation still apply in our contemporary communities. Other reasons we pay little attention to. For example, as Christians we know that we should not base people's status in the community on their marital status. Both married and single people are equally valuable, complete, and competent members of the community.

Still, we desire to get married. This chapter is not intended to negate the traditional set-up for marriages, but to add onto beliefs your community might hold. If there is a disagreement between traditional cultural beliefs and biblical beliefs, this chapter also intends to highlight those differences and guide you in making decisions.

In our interaction with married couples and individuals desiring to get married, we have heard several common reasons in our modern set-up. These include:

Living together legally. "We are in a *come-we-stay* (cohabiting) relationship. I really love her and I don't mind continuing like this, but she says she wants to make it legal. If that is what she wants, we'll go ahead and do it."

We are of age. "We are not growing young any more. His father keeps reminding him that as the oldest child in the family, he needs to get married to open the door for the rest of his siblings."

Loneliness. "It gets lonely sometimes. So many of my friends are married already. It will be nice to have someone to share my life with."

Financial security. "It really is a win-win arrangement. When we bring our two salaries together, we can afford a lot more. We will enjoy the security that comes with having two incomes."

Guilt-free sex. "We look forward to having sex without feeling as guilty as we do now sometimes, especially when we are at church and feel we are reminded that we are 'living in sin.'"

Our Story

I, James, got married in my early 30s. For a while, my family wondered if I was ever going to get married. They felt that I was growing old. While I also desired to marry, I knew I needed to wait until I met the right person. Thankfully, my involvement in sports, church activities, and personal development helped me go through seasons when I felt lonely. It would have been easier for me to make a rushed decision had

I not been actively involved in my community or had personal goals I was working towards.

When I met Chao and when we agreed to get married, we did not think through biblical reasons for our marriage. But we had some practical ideas about why marriage was good for us. We felt we were of mature age to make the decision. We knew it was time for us to go through this rite of passage and to have children who would also carry our family name forward. We hoped that when we put two heads together, two incomes together, and two families together, we were likely to have a richer life than if we remained single. Marriage would also provide us with companionship and protect us from loneliness.

Our reasons weren't bad. While age alone is not a good enough reason to get married, it is important to make the decision to get married when you are of mature age. Marriage also relieves the pang of loneliness. Two people give each other the companionship that human beings desire and were created for. And yes, sharing some responsibilities, including financial responsibilities, could make life a lot easier for the couple as they bring two incomes together. However, when we later became intentional about building our marriage, we came to better understand God's purpose for marriage. This gave our marriage a deeper meaning and enriched it. Your reasons for getting married now and to this person should be grounded in these deeper reasons for marriage.

What Are the Reasons God Initiated Marriage?

God put Adam and Eve together as husband and wife for several reasons. These reasons shape a Christian perspective on marriage and guide us in our decisions to give and take in marriage.

Companionship

Before there were social clubs, gyms, churches, schools, and even workplaces where people find others to interact with, God formally instituted companionship. In the garden, Adam had work to do with responsibility over all the creatures and the land that God had given him. While he had the company of animals, they could not meet his need for companionship. Prior to this, God would create and then he would say, "It is good." But for the first time in his creation act, God said, "It is *not good* for the man to be alone. I will make a helper suitable for him" (Genesis 2:18, emphasis added). So, God in his power created Adam with a need that could not be met by himself or anything that surrounded him. He needed the company of someone who could complement him. Thus God fashioned Eve so that they could spend time together, offer camaraderie to each other, and build intimacy. Marriage is therefore a promise to be someone's companion. As a man, just like Adam, you will receive the companionship of the woman you are marrying as a gift from God. And women, we believe your future husband is God's gift to you too! This companionship is not only for physical closeness, it is also for mental, emotional, and spiritual closeness.

Reflecting the Image of God

In Genesis 1:26-27, God said, "Let us make mankind *in our image, in our likeness*, so that they may rule over the fish in the sea and the birds in the sky, over the livestock and all the wild animals, and over all the creatures that move along the ground" (emphasis added). The word *our* here indicates that God is one God in essence, who functions in three persons – the Father, the Son, and the Holy Spirit. Yet these persons are united, and God does not contradict himself.

One way we reflect the image of God is in marriage. In marriage, God puts two very different people together, and they become one in unity. Marriage always involves people of two genders. It also often involves differences of ethnic groups, cultures, regions, socio-economic status, or denominations. But God's power and beauty are displayed as a couple reflects an image of the unity of God the Father, the Son, and the Holy Spirit.

Sometimes God seems far away, distant, and strange to the natural eye. A beautiful, God-centred marriage is like a telescope. Through the telescope of marriage, some of the attributes of God that are not visible to the naked eye seem closer and easier to understand. God's intention is that when we look into a marriage, we see a testimony of the unity of God the Father, the Son, and the Holy Spirit. His intention is that we see the testimony of God's truth, power, beauty, and greatness. This union of diversity proclaims to the world that in Christ there is "neither Jew nor Gentile, neither slave nor free, nor is there male and female, for you are all one in Christ Jesus" (Galatians 3:28).

Another way our marriages reflect God's image is by the love and forgiveness we demonstrate in our relationship with each other. There are people in your circle who will not go to church or seek a relationship with God. But they will watch you in your marriage. As you choose to love like God in your marriage, you will be bringing God himself to them. Do not be surprised when, as they watch you, they come and ask you to tell them what your secret is.

Build a Godly Legacy

In marriage, couples can be fruitful by raising children who will continue with the legacy that God initiated in their parents. Just after creating man and woman, God said, "Be fruitful and increase in number; fill the earth and subdue it" (Genesis 1:28). In Deuteronomy 6:5-7, God explains that his most important commandment must be passed along to our children:

> Love the Lord your God with all your heart and with all your soul and with all your strength. These commandments that I give you today are to be on your hearts. Impress them on your children. Talk about them when you sit at home and when you walk along the road, when you lie down and when you get up.

God's purpose for marriage is that his legacy will continue through the children you impact as a couple. As God blesses you with children, you are to intentionally prepare them to be ambassadors of the message of God to the world. This purpose is not only for those whom God will give children to carry in their wombs, but also for couples who will have children by other ways, including adoption, guardianship, or caring for other children they interact with. A couple must be intentional to accomplish God's purpose to continue his ministry through the children they nurture. When the children are of age and have their own children, they will also do the same.

Many in our culture will understand the importance of leaving an inheritance to your children. Before my father (James) died, he put his house in order by allocating every property he had to one of his children. He gave us an inheritance that he hoped we would steward and one day pass on to our children. Chao and I are, therefore, recipients of this inheritance and one day, we hope to pass it on to our children.

My father also passed on to me and my siblings a legacy of salvation and service to God. He was intentional in evangelizing his own people, beginning with his wife and his children. By the time he was dying, he had heard each one of his children confess Jesus as their Lord and Saviour.

The material inheritance that my father gave to each one of his children can be sold, stolen by corrupt people, or grabbed by other family members. The godly legacy that my father left, on the other hand, is an inheritance that lasts. A godly legacy is a privilege every believer has. In turn, every believer is responsible to pass it on to someone else, beginning with one's own children. As you prepare for marriage, look forward to telling the world about Jesus through the children God will give you and those he will have you reach out to.

Are You Ready for Marriage?

Now that we have discussed some of God's purposes for marriage, you are in a position to think through the decision you are about to make.

The first question to ask is whether you know the God who created marriage. Are you both pursuing God individually and together? This is the best way to understand what marriage is and be equipped with all you will need in your marriage journey. In a later chapter, we will discuss your individual relationship with God. You will have the opportunity to consider this relationship and if there are decisions you need to make about this relationship, you will have that opportunity.

As you reflect on God's purposes for marriage, you can benefit by asking yourself questions on your readiness. Some of the questions include the following:

1. Do I want to get married? Do I want to marry this person? Do I want to marry him or her now?
2. Why do I want to get married?
3. Why do I want to marry this person?
4. Am I prepared to live out God's purposes for my marriage with the one I intend to marry?
5. Are there areas in my life that I need to take care of before I get married?
6. Is there anything in our relationship or with me as an individual that, if not dealt with now, would make it difficult for us to live out God's purposes for our marriage?
7. If I have any reservations about getting married now or to this person, can I be honest with myself and with my intended spouse?

Be Aware of Red Flags

In addition to asking yourself questions about your decision to get married, you need to be aware of and work through some serious areas of concern. Read through these carefully and think about whether any of them apply to you.

Feeling pressured to get married quickly. This pressure can come from family members or from your culture. Your family may feel that you are of age and so you need to hurry up and marry. This is especially true when they believe you are almost past the childbearing age and that you need to quickly have children. Your culture may also make you feel that you are incomplete until you get married. As a result, one or both of you may be rushing into marriage.

Spiritual incompatibility. Perhaps one of you is committed to following Christ, but the other has not committed to call him Lord and Saviour. It could be that one of you has made a commitment to be intentional in your spiritual growth, but the other has lost interest in fellowship with God and is pursuing other priorities. Spiritual incompatibility makes it difficult for both of you to live out God's purposes for marriage because you are not grounded on the same foundation.

Financial health. Are you habitually spending more than you have? Perhaps you are in debt and have no plan to pay it off. It could be one of you is not able to hold a job and depends on others to make ends meet. Your parents may be dependent on you and expect you to be their primary provider even after you get married. Finances are one of the most common causes of conflict in marriages, so it is best to resolve these issues before you get married.

Resolving conflicts. When you have a conflict, do you discuss the problem? Are one or both of you reluctant to discuss it and, instead, just wish it away? Do one or both of you keep quiet to appease the other? Do either of you respond in anger that you find difficult to control?

Your past. Are you dealing with fears from your past, whether from your family of origin or any previous relationships? If your parents' marriage was difficult, are you feeling handicapped by fears that yours could end up like theirs? Is this fear clouding your decisions? Are you afraid to be honest with each other out of fear that the other person will react or be unable to deal with your honesty?

Habits or addictions. Are there any bad habits that you find hard or even unwilling to break? Do you use addictive substances? Do you find it hard to go without a drink or something else you love? Do you look at pornography? Do you have other sexual habits that you are ashamed of?

As you read through the red flags, does anything catch your eye? It is wise to take time to work through those difficulties. At the end of the chapter, you will have the opportunity to reflect on and work through these. If you have a mentor couple, don't be afraid to share with them. They can walk with you or refer you to professionals who can help. You can also seek help in your church. Even if your church does not have a counselling ministry, they can support you in prayer, help you find help, and keep you accountable.

Mercy and Victor

Mercy and Victor still share how helpful it was that they chose to work through their red flags before they got married.

The couple came to us wounded and discouraged by the challenges they faced. Victor's parents did not want any of their children to marry into Mercy's tribe. Also, Mercy would get paid and give the money to her parents. They determined how much of her income she needed and would keep the rest for themselves. However, Victor and Mercy were determined to fight and make right what they could before they got married. Our mutual friends referred them to us, hoping they could be mentored as they prepared for their marriage.

We encouraged them to invite a relative and other people they admired to speak to their parents on their behalf. Mercy and Victor cried together and fought together. They ended up postponing their wedding date so they could have more time, with the help of relatives and others they involved, to work out the tribal issue with Victor's parents. During this break, they also agreed to set financial boundaries with Mercy's parents. In the end, Victor's parents came around. While Mercy's parents were reluctant to let go of their control on her finances, Mercy made it clear that going into marriage, she and Victor would be responsible for both their finances and give to her parents what they both agreed. When we attended Victor and Mercy's wedding, we rejoiced as we watched both their parents publicly bless their children's union.

More than eight years later, you can tell that Mercy and Victor have learned to stand together as a team and put God first in their marriage. Now they are celebrating God's purpose for their marriage!

Conclusion

As James and I (Chao) have worked with couples from different walks of life, we have discovered that when couples understand why they got married in the first place, they are more willing to build, enjoy, celebrate, and stay in their marriage. When they are faced with conflicts, when the pressures of life seem unbearable, when hard circumstances come their way, they fight together and hold up their marriage. They still work towards companionship with each other, mirroring God's image, and continuing to build a godly legacy in their home.

As the two of you understand and embrace God's purpose for marriage, you are more prepared for that day when you will exchange your vows and begin to build your marriage on God's foundation.

Intergenerational Marriages

In our African traditions, it was common for an older man to marry a much younger wife. Polygamy was part of the culture and, therefore, the wife or wives that came after the first were significantly younger than the husband. Additionally, because of lack of quick medical intervention in risky pregnancies and deliveries, it was more common than it is now for the first wife to die during pregnancy or childbirth. Even today, especially after a man is widowed or divorced, it is common for the man to remarry a wife who is significantly younger than him.

Intergenerational marriages have several advantages. When the man is older, it can be assumed that he is more mature and stable in his life, including financially. He has learned how to deal with life's trials. This fact can also lead to unique challenges in a marriage. While the man may be seasoned in life, he may not have the patience or the know-how to give his young bride room to grow through the different seasons in her life. He may be settled in his ways, which could mean the young bride will not have the joy of exploring and learning with her husband. It will take a great deal of patience and intentionality for both spouses to appreciate their generational differences and build their own unique culture.

While financial stability is often a plus in a relationship, finances may pose a bigger challenge depending on how the man ended his last marriage. Negotiating with or even fighting a first wife over finances can cause great heartache. Navigating his relationship with his children from a previous relationship can be difficult for the young wife. If the younger wife has children with the husband, they will be brought into pre-existing conflicts.

Sometimes it is also difficult for one or both family members to accept an intergenerational marriage. Some families may feel that the young bride is a "gold digger" trying to access the wealth the man worked so hard for. While we cannot predict what health challenges will hit a marriage, a home where the bride is much younger means she may not have as many active years with her husband before she begins to care for him as an elderly person. She might feel that she has her whole life ahead of her, yet she has to hold off to take care of her ageing husband.

While intergenerational marriages do not happen as much where the man is younger than the woman, we cannot discount them completely. In some cultures, these types of arrangements are loosely viewed as the young man finding a *sponsor*. While most of these arrangements are short-lived – the one seeking *sponsorship* terminates the relationship, once they have achieved their goal – some of these relationships continue in marriage. Someone getting married in this type of arrangement should seek to understand how their marriage will accomplish God's purpose for marriage using the principles we described above.

If you are considering an intergenerational marriage, it is important to think through the unique aspects of your marriage and be intentional to work through them. Take some time, too, to revisit the biblical reasons for marriage in this chapter. How, even in your unique situation, will you intentionally live out God's purpose for your marriage?

Digging Deeper

Individual Reflection

Find a quiet place with some privacy to complete this section.

1. Look at the list of red flags in this chapter. Do you feel concerned about any area that you, your intended other, or both of you need to work on? Are there any other areas of concern to you that are not listed?

   If at all possible, take a personal retreat and work through those areas of concern. If the red flags are things you have noticed about yourself, write them down. Write down some of the solutions or the help you need to resolve those areas. If the areas regard your intended other, note them down. Pray specifically for wisdom on how to confront the issues when you come back together.
2. If, after looking through the suggested red flags, you do not find any major area of concern, then go back to the **Are you ready for marriage?** section on **page 41**. Take time to reflect on the list of questions about your readiness. Write down your responses and be ready to share with your intended other.

Prayer

Before you start, spend time praying that you both will be open to listening to each other.

Discussion

Meet together and complete this section. Make sure you choose a place where you can talk uninterrupted.

Take turns sharing what you learned from your reflections or during your retreat, making sure you are specific about the areas of concern for both yourself and for your intended other.

Agree on a next step as you move forward.

Mentors

Share any red flags or questions about readiness that either of you noticed.

How specifically do you need your mentors to help you work through this or keep you accountable? If your mentor couple thinks professional help would be appropriate, ask them to help you identify your next step to finding that help. If they recommend a place or person, take down the information and follow up.

Take It Further

Do the **Couples Interview** from the Activities and Resources section on pages 183-184.

One of the ways we learn about marriage is by listening to couples who are already married. One way to listen authentically is to ask specific questions. This exercise is meant to do exactly that.

Find two couples you look up to who have been married for at least five years. One of the couples could be your mentors. Other couples could be those you know from your church or other social groups. Find a comfortable place to visit over tea or a light meal. Go prepared to take notes, ask questions, and enjoy the visit. When you are done with the interview, make time where the two of you can sit and discuss some of your take-aways from the interview with the couples.

4

How To Become One

Jabali and his dad were not just father and son, they were also good friends. They often spent Sunday afternoons watching football together. "You know my team always beats yours!" Jabali would tease.

"You wish!" his father would reply.

So when Jabali's father asked for a meeting, Jabali was happy to make time. They met at the restaurant at the corner between Jabali's workplace and the bank his parents frequented. Thankfully, the lunch crowd had not built up yet. "Let me buy you lunch," Jabali said as he sat in the corner.

"They serve real food here, not the food you young people like to eat nowadays," Jabali's dad said with a smile.

After their food came, Jabali's father said, "Son, my days with you as a single man are numbered. I want to take every opportunity I have to spend time with you before you start your own family. I know you can't understand now, but marriage changes a lot of things in a man's life." After a few more niceties, Jabali's father pulled out an envelope. "I have waited for a long time to give this to you, son. Your mother wanted me to wait until after your wedding, but I don't see much reason to wait. When I was about to get married, my father called me one day and did this same thing to me." His voice failed as his eyes began filling with tears. "I hope that the Lord will keep you, give you sons and daughters, and that one day you will get to do the same with them."

Jabali was not used to seeing his father share his emotions openly. He did not know how to respond. He squeezed his father's shoulders. He opened the envelope to find a title deed for a piece of land next to his parents' house.

Before Jabali could respond, his father said, "Next week we can go by the ministry of lands and start the process of transferring the deed to your name. Do with it as you wish."

While Jabali knew that one day his father would have this kind of conversation with him, he never expected to receive an inheritance this early in his life. Jabali stood and embraced his father. "I did not expect this." He looked his dad in the eye and said with a smile, "I sure hope you're not thinking of dying soon."

His father laughed. "Don't worry, we have a long time to wait before that day comes!"

Jabali could not wait to share the news with Karembo that evening. They had already agreed to meet after work at a coffee shop near her home. Jabali said, "I am not really hungry for food. I am full with some news that I know you will be happy to hear." Then Jabali told

Karembo of the surprise his dad had for him. "You know what this means! Instead of looking for an apartment, we can put together the money we have and put up a one-bedroom as we slowly build our dream house."

Karembo raised her eyebrows and then let out a loud laugh. She hugged herself, then stood and hugged Jabali. "Wow! Jabali, this is a wonderful thing. I can't believe it is happening to us!"

Owning a piece of land in the city was a desire not many people saw fulfilled. Building a house at such a tender age sounded thrilling – and daunting. As Karembo celebrated the news, she also privately worried. "Am I ready to live this close to my in-laws? What if it ends up being the most terrible thing we ever did?" That night, she dreamed that Jabali's mother was in her kitchen making a meal for "my son". She was relieved to wake up and find it was a dream.

How Two Become One Flesh

In getting married, the two of you are choosing to place your marriage relationship above any other human relationship. So as you prepare for your marriage, both of you are also preparing to loosen ties to your parents, family members, friends, and some other commitments so that you can join together and build unity in your marriage. While you both will always be tied to your families of origin and belong in relationships with others, marriage calls you to respectfully and wisely transfer your loyalties from your parents to your spouse. You are making a new allegiance.

Genesis 2:24 describes what happens when people get married. Let's examine it closely to learn some principles for how you create a strong union. The verse says: "Therefore a man shall leave his father and his mother and hold fast to his wife, and they shall become one flesh" (ESV).

Leaving

The first step is leaving: "Therefore a man shall leave his father and his mother …"

Getting married is like a transfer of citizenship from one nationality to another. Just as each nation has its constitution, a marriage also has its constitution. When one becomes a citizen of a nation, he pledges allegiance to that nation and to what it stands for. So is it with marriage – you move from being loyal to your family of birth and close friends and other relationships, to pledging your loyalty first to your spouse. We call this transfer of loyalty *leaving*. Leaving involves both of you intentionally letting go of your dependence, comfort, and security with your parents, to build dependence, comfort, and security with your spouse. Loosening the ties that bind you to your parents enables you to protect both your marriage and your relationships with your family.

The first way you separate is physically. For instance, you need to decide together where to live when you get married. As Jabali and Karembo were realizing, living close to either of your families of origin has its joys and challenges. The couple who lives in the same compound or street with their family can drop in on each other unannounced. This can work for or against you. If your parents are elderly or have health challenges, they may ask a lot of you. When you have a young family or need urgent favours, living close to your family can work to your advantage. On the other hand, some couples live in the city while their parents live in the village, but they still struggle to maintain boundaries. It is common to find parents calling their children at the end of the month, reminding them of their responsibility to support them financially. Wherever you choose to live, you will need to agree as a couple to create the physical space you need to define yourselves and build your marriage and your home. Build not only a physical home, but also an emotionally healthy home where you both feel affirmed and comfortable.

Leaving physically makes room for the two of you to leave socially and emotionally. You or your parents may have depended on each other to fill the social and emotional void. Now you will need to learn to do that as a couple, while also agreeing how best you can continue to be involved with your family members. Sometimes couples have had their social and emotional needs met by families of choice, such as the church family, social networks from workplaces, friends, and other extended family members. New couples need to be aware that these families of choice should help build the marriage, not tear it down. For instance, you may find one spouse more committed to the church than the other. That spouse quickly becomes part of that church family. The other spouse may begin to feel left out. Instead of making decisions as a couple, the churchgoer takes guidance from the church leader and ignores her or his spouse's involvement. Take care that your outside relationships build your unity and, when necessary, take the necessary steps to leave socially and emotionally. It makes it easier when you as a couple are connected to common friends, the same church, and other social networks.

While we will discuss the topic of finances further in a later chapter, we want to mention here that depending financially on your parents, or them depending on you, can also cause a problem. There is nothing wrong with receiving financial gifts from your family members or loaning each other money. However, be careful that your agreement does not bind you to others and shift your priority away from your spouse.

Challenges to Leaving

We shouldn't take lightly the idea of two becoming one. The Bible states the power of leaving and becoming one, so it is important for you to see what it should look like as you begin your marriage union.

However, we often find in our work with couples that this is one of the most challenging principles to live out. Let's look at some reasons why people find it difficult.

Is Leaving un-African?

In our African cultures, where living in community is key to everyone's welfare and the extended family is important for the strength of a home, the Bible might seem to contradict our culture when it says, "Therefore a man shall leave his father and his mother and hold fast to his wife, and they shall become one flesh" (Genesis 2:24, ESV). Thankfully, these words were spoken to a culture similar to ours. Moses wrote about the Garden of Eden culture, addressing the Hebrew community who held on to communal living. The only "I" that they held on to was the "I AM" who was Yahweh their God. Everything else was about "we." And yet they chose to live as God had commanded them, where husband and wife, still part of the community, prioritized their marriage before any other relationship. In so doing, they became one flesh. As they strengthened their marriage union, they were, in effect, strengthening the unity of the community.

For example, God told Abram, "Go from your country, your people and your father's household to the land I will show you" (Genesis 12:1). So he and Sarah left for Canaan. God made it clear that Abraham's obedience to leave and build a future with Sarah, a future that was different from those in his community, was tied to God's promises to him, to his people, and to generations to come. As you read the story of Abraham, you see that in moments when he and Sarah obeyed God, their obedience benefited not only their immediate family, but the entire community.

As you take the space to get to know each other and determine your values as a couple, you are able to influence the rest of your family and the community for everyone's good.

When It Is Hard to Leave

Sometimes circumstances make it feel difficult, or even impossible, to leave socially, emotionally, or financially. Still, you can find ways as a couple to agree how you are going to support your family together, while also agreeing how you will protect your union and growth together in your marriage. Listen to a couple we counselled whom we'll call Kadogo and Michael as they describe how they navigated this challenge.

Kadogo and Michael had not been married long before they realized they were growing apart.

Michael said, "My father died about six months before Kadogo and I got married. As we prepared for our marriage, I divided my time between work, my mother, and Kadogo. My mother has struggled to adjust to life without my father, so I have tried to help make her a bit more comfortable. I have especially gone over to her house in the evening to eat with her, ensure she was eating well, and give her company."

Kadogo said, "I met Michael's mum during one of her hardest seasons in life. Michael's father had already been battling a terminal disease when Michael introduced me to them. Since his father's death, I have tried to support his mum, Michael, and his siblings as much as I could. I wished we could spend more time together, especially in the evening after work when both of us had more time. But I understood that Michael's mother could do with the company of her loved ones. But after we married and moved into our own place, I thought that would change. Instead, he continues to go over to spend several evenings eating with his mother. I have lost count of the number of times I have waited for Michael to eat together with me. When he gets home, he tells me he has already eaten with his mother. I feel like Michael's allegiance is first towards his mother. When will he have time for his bride? I don't want Michael to think I was being insensitive to his mother, so for the longest time I have not said anything."

Michael said, "Sometimes I try to eat a bit less at Mother's house and plan to eat something with Kadogo. But when I get home, the house is empty and the kitchen looks as clean as it was when we left for work!"

Kadogo responded, "I have gotten to a point where I feel that I may as well do my own thing, since he is busy taking care of his mother. So sometimes I make my own evening arrangements with family and friends, and I do not share my plans with Michael."

Our African Parents

Michael's sense of obligation towards his parent is something most of us recognize with our parents. Our parents sacrificed to help us succeed and have a better life than they did. We know stories of mothers breaking their backs to fend for their children and fathers taking up manual jobs or selling property to pay for school fees. Having watched our parents give up their dreams for us drives many of us, after we have our education and secure jobs, to make sure our parents do not suffer the same pain we saw them suffer when we were growing up. Not only do we work hard to make their lives more comfortable, we try as much as we can to involve them in our lives. Sometimes, we invite them to speak into different areas of our lives, including our marriages.

The problem comes when a son or daughter is so connected with a parent that even when they get married, they do not let go of dependence between them and their parents. An unhealthy dependence between parents and children can lead to a breakdown of a marriage. Families can tear the couple apart instead of helping them stay glued together. In Matthew 19:6, Jesus says of marriage, "Therefore what God has joined together, let no one separate." While in the original context, Jesus was referring to divorce breaking a union that God created, we believe it applies to anything that can cause the breakdown of a marriage covenant before God.

While your parents may not have the language to express it right now, they want you to succeed not only in your marriage but also in raising your children to have access to more than you had access to. To succeed, you will need to prioritize unity in your marriage. You have the joy of both of you agreeing to speak as one and teaching your parents what that looks like in your new home.

Holding Fast

Genesis 2:24 describes the next step as holding fast to your spouse. After you have chosen to leave your mother and father physically, emotionally, socially, and financially, you begin to hold fast to one another in your marriage. Neither leaving nor holding fast happens overnight, but you have to be willing to start the process.

In some Bible translations, holding fast is referred to as *cleaving*. Cleaving doesn't mean that the two of you should spend every minute together, never disagree, or have no meaningful relationships outside of your marriage. Cleaving means that you vow to stand together, to remain steadfast, and to closely pursue each other even when things are not going well or are not as clear as you would like.

One way to solidify your unity is by praying together. Prayer forms a bond that is difficult to break. It not only strengthens your intimacy with each other, it also strengthens your intimacy with God. When you cleave to each other, you choose to resolve differences when they come up. You choose to practice patience with each other, and seek and grant forgiveness. Cleaving means choosing to make God the centre of your marriage, as both of you continuously seek the counsel of God in his Word and in the people he has placed around you. Cleaving means you are willing to team up and build a unique culture together.

Kadogo and Michael

We listened to Michael and Kadogo and asked them some questions.

"Michael, have you asked your mother if this is the best way you can support her?"

Michael said, "I guess I don't remember a time I asked her how we, as her children, could be there for her. I got into the habit of spending more and more time with my mother. It feels that if I don't, she will fall apart."

"Could your other siblings play a role in supporting her?"

"I am the oldest in the family, so I feel I need to lead in this area. I expected my other two siblings to help, but I suppose I have not sat them down and tried to agree how they should also be involved in keeping our mother company. I want us to show her that, with our father gone, she still has us."

We said, "Kadogo, it sounds like you want to support his mother. But you feel the way you are doing it now is pulling you apart. How could you support her in a way that brings you together?"

"I can see us committing to go by her house for dinner once a week together for now. Maybe after a while we would do it a lot less," Kadogo said.

We asked, "It is possible that if you didn't visit every day, your mother might enjoy a quiet meal alone? Perhaps she would prefer to invite her own friends."

By the end of this discussion, Michael and Kadogo had agreed that visiting Michael's mother once a week together would help them grow together as a couple. They also agreed to give Michael's mother the opportunity to give feedback about what she needed, rather than what Michael thought she needed. Michael said, "Who knows, maybe she has felt crowded, but hasn't said anything because she does not want to make me feel bad."

Becoming One Flesh

After you choose to leave and hold fast to each other, becoming one flesh becomes possible. This happens when both man and woman begin to think as one, to act as one, and to also choose to be together physically. The sexual union is an important part of becoming one. It is also not the only glue that unites a couple. In Ephesians 5:28-31, Paul describes how a husband and wife build such an intimate relationship that whatever the man does for himself, good or bad, he also does it for her because the two have become one flesh.

The next verse in Genesis 2 describes the intimacy between Adam and Eve: "Adam and his wife were both naked, and they felt no shame." (2:25). Adam and Eve were perfectly open and transparent with each other. They exercised vulnerability with one another. While we never fully achieve this now that sin has entered the world, we can glimpse this in marriage when two people are so comfortable with each other that nothing, not even their clothes, can come between them. Our prayer for you is that you would experience the blessing of intimacy in your union as you become one.

Kadogo and Michael

Michael and Kadogo were able to express their desire to have a meal with his mother once a week, or every so often, if she preferred it that way.

"How did it go?" we asked.

"I could see my mother was a bit uneasy when she heard I would not be stopping by her house as often because she had gotten used to seeing me," Michael said. "I had also gotten used to spending time with her. I would be lying if I said I would not miss those moments with her and the way it made me feel to know I was being responsible for her. But I know Kadogo is the wife I chose to marry, and she and I have a lifetime together. We need to start building our home together," Michael said.

Kadogo reported in our session, "The last time we stopped to see Michael's mother, she was happy to have us over. As we left to go to our place, she said, 'OK kids, I have some plans with my friends the next two weeks. Don't worry about coming by to check on me or to eat with me. Go on and do what newlyweds do!'" Kadogo said this with a smile at Michael.

Conclusion

When you choose to leave your mother and father, you are severing the umbilical cord – physically, emotionally, socially, and financially – so that you can build your marriage. This does not mean you cannot be there for your parents. Families are a strong support system in a marriage relationship, and it would be unwise for a couple getting married to walk away from their family. You have a common background with your family members, and when you do not have them in your life, you deny yourself something meaningful and beautiful. You can still consider blessing your family first, before you bless others outside your family. However, a delicate, healthy balance needs to be forged for the new couple to leave and still keep a healthy relationship with their family. Remember, as you build each other, you are able to help build others in your circles.

Digging Deeper

Individual Reflection

Find a quiet place with some privacy to complete this section.

1. Take stock of your physical, social, emotional, and financial ties. What are some areas that could potentially hinder you from working towards becoming one?
2. As you think about "leaving", with whom else, aside from family members, do you need to sever the umbilical cord?
3. Couples often find it difficult to cleave to each other because they are not willing to let go of what is familiar to them. It could be late night social gatherings, women's meetings every Saturday, or meals at their parents' homes. What might you find difficult to let go of?
4. Think about your social relationships. How do they build or compromise your closeness as a couple?

Discussion

Meet together and complete this section. Make sure you choose a place where you can talk uninterrupted.

1. Share your answers to the questions above with each other.
2. What are the rewards of holding fast and becoming one?
3. What will it take for you to keep healthy relational boundaries with your parents, close family members, and friends?

Prayer

Finish your time together by praying for unity in your marriage, physically, socially, emotionally, spiritually, and financially.

Mentors

Share with your mentor couple how you intend to keep healthy relationship boundaries with your parents, close family members, and friends. What steps do you plan to take?

Take It Further

Look at the **Parents Interview** in the Activities and Resources section on pages 185-186.

This questionnaire is for you to give to your parents or the guardians who raised you. You can gain insight on yourself through the eyes of the people who have known you the most. Their perspective can bring to light anything you need to work through as you get into your marriage.

Are You Considering Polygamy?

Some African countries recognize and allow polygamy as a form of marriage in their constitutions. It is possible that you or someone you know is considering getting into a polygamous relationship. As a woman, you may be considering getting married to a man who is already married. As a man, you may be considering adding an additional wife to your home now or sometime in the future.

In this session, we have focused on how two become one. As you consider having more than one wife or as you consider being a co-wife, how do you plan to build oneness in this set-up?

The Old Testament records polygamous unions, but they are never portrayed as the ideal. In Genesis 2:24, one man leaves his parents and is joined to one wife. This is what marriage was like when things were as God intended for them to be, before the Fall in Genesis 3. From there on, in Genesis 4:19, the Bible records that Lamech married two wives. The Israelites lived among other cultures and they adopted customs, including marriage customs, from cultures around them. Later on, others including Abraham, Jacob, David, and Solomon took more than one wife. Each one of these marriages is recorded as having challenges that were directly related to their polygamous nature. In the New Testament, Paul speaks of deacons and elders being husbands of one wife. Paul, also in Ephesians 5, uses the analogy of Christ's oneness with the church as a model for a husband's union with his wife.

This brief information is to help you make decisions with understanding. You might have a lot more questions regarding polygamy. Do not be afraid to approach your pastor or other respected Christians in your community and openly ask those questions. Go back to the Bible and choose to be a student on this subject. Highlight anything you might have a question about, and when you meet with any of those leaders, take them to the Bible so that your discussion will be guided by the passages.

Are You Marrying into a Blended Family?

As you go through this manual, this may not be the first marriage for one or both of you. You may be divorced or widowed. You also may be coming into marriage with children either from a past relationship or marriage. If one or both of you already have children from your past, you are beginning life with more than just the two of you. If the other parent to your children is still involved in the raising of those children, you will be co-parenting and building a unique culture that will look different for you.

If you are coming in with this unique situation, it is important that first and foremost you remember God's love for you and his expectation for your marriage is no less than for the ones getting married for the first time. God's message about marriage is the same; the method on how to "leave" and "cleave" is what may be different. Seek to find resources that speak to your unique situation. It is highly likely that other couples in your circle married under situations similar to yours. Reach out to them. You can learn from each other and help each other find resources. Don't ignore the fact that you are beginning your marriage differently from couples who are both getting married for the first time or getting married without children. But don't allow this to be a crutch that holds you back from "leaving" and "cleaving". By God's grace, you can still do it.

5

Communicating through Conflict

Now that they had their own piece of land, Jabali and Karembo agreed to find out what it would take to build a house on their plot. "You never know, we could put up a house and move in before our wedding," they dreamed. They had a friend who was a builder, so they stopped by to see him at the site where he was working. They found him under a tree, drinking tea on his break.

"So this is where you hide from the hot sun, is it, Kevo?"

"Jabali, my man! Karembo, hello. How are you? How are your parents?"

Jabali answered, "We are all well. Just getting ready for the big day! I sent you the invitation card and you better show up! But enough about that, right now I want you to hear some exciting news! My dad has given us a plot of land next to his house."

“Really?” Kevo responded with a hearty laugh.

“We were thinking of slowly building on our new plot,” Jabali said.

“That’s awesome! I happen to know a good builder,” Kevo laughed as he pointed his thumb towards his chest.

“We were wondering if you could come up with some cost estimates for us. We have only six months to the wedding, so we are crunched on both time and money.”

“Six months? I am good at my job, but I am not a miracle worker! I don’t think a house could be ready for someone to move in that quickly. Do you have somewhere to live in the meantime as you wait?” Kevo asked.

Karembo frowned. She put her hands on her head and moved a bit further from Jabali and Kevo. Jabali said without hesitation, “We can stay at my parents’ adjacent room that they built for their workers. It is self-contained. I’ll talk to my dad and let him know of our plans. So now, can we start talking about those cost estimates? I can’t wait to build a house for my soon-to-be-bride,” Jabali said as he turned to pull Karembo back to the conversation.

Before Jabali could pull Karembo closer, she pulled him towards her and whispered, “What are you doing? Are you serious? Where did that come from? Can we talk about this first?”

“Well, man, I will let the two of you talk, and I will be right here when you make a decision. It’s good to see you and congratulations on your upcoming wedding. I will definitely be there.” Kevo gave Jabali a pat on his back and shook Karembo’s hand, then walked back to the shade, picked up his tea mug and headed over to the construction site. Karembo hurriedly shook Kevo’s hand and went and sat in the car. She felt her heart beating faster than it normally did. Her hands were shaking, and she could feel the beginnings of a headache. Jabali opened the car door, whistling a tune and turned on his favourite music.

As they turned the corner that took them to Karembo's parents' house, she could not stay quiet for any longer. "Had you planned all along that we would start our lives together at your parents' house? Did you ever consider how I would feel about such an arrangement? How could you? And you even told the builder about your plans before we talked about them. I thought we had agreed we would be making decisions together?" Karembo kept on. She was not waiting for Jabali to respond. She wanted him to hear everything she had to say. Jabali tried to respond but the more he tried, the louder and longer she spoke. "I can't believe you did this," she said.

"Karembo, can you let me explain? I am sorry I let the words escape my lips before we talked about this. But this is a good and practical solution. I am doing this for us. But from the look of things, you are not even appreciating what I am doing to build us a home." As they parked in front of the house, their yelling drowned out almost every word the other said.

Karembo threw her hands in the air and exclaimed, "I can't take this anymore. You never listen to me!" With that, she strode away and left Jabali still trying to finish talking.

He jumped out of the car. "Karembo, let me explain!" He tried to catch up, but she had already climbed the steps to her parents' house. "Please don't walk out on me!" Karembo let the door slam shut behind her. Jabali could not follow Karembo into the house. He stood outside the car for a few minutes, hoping she would walk back out. He hit the steering wheel with his fist. *Where do we even go from here?*

Conflict Is Inevitable

Conflict in a relationship is inevitable. Two very different people are joining together with many differences, so conflicts are as natural as breathing air. You should not aim to avoid conflict, but to communicate effectively through conflict. The goal in your communication is to strengthen the bond between the two of you and close any gap that the conflict has caused. That is why you need to be intentional when you are communicating with each other.

In this chapter, couples will learn the importance of authentic and intentional communication, the key to getting successfully to the other side of conflict.

How Do Couples Deal with Conflict?

Win

Often people enter a conflict with the goal of proving that they are right, getting their way, or justifying themselves. This approach to conflict is focused on winning the argument. Fighting to win may seem a quick way to end the conflict. Unfortunately, it often makes the situation worse because the issue is not dealt with. More importantly, when we fight to win, we forget the powerful principle of unity where two become one. In Ephesians 5:28, Paul instructs husbands to "love their wives as their own bodies. He who loves his wife loves himself." Genesis 2:24 speaks of a couple who will "become one flesh." If two of you have become one flesh, what you do to the other person you also do to yourself. Fighting against your spouse is actually fighting yourself. If one wins and the other one loses, it means that both lose. While it is important to acknowledge how each person feels, ultimately it is not about who wins and who loses. It is about what is right and what grows the relationship.

Yield

Sometimes one person in a relationship is tired of fighting over an issue. He or she may wish the topic had never been brought up and that things could go back to how they were before. The person may choose to give up on their views and let the other person have their way. Yielding may provide the opportunity for either or both of you to look at the situation from a different angle. However, if it is done too often, it does not equip you as a couple for future conflict resolutions.

If you yield, you just sweep your problems under the rug. At some point, you will need to go back to the carpet and clean it up. If you allow the dirt to keep piling up, the pile of dirt will become overwhelming. The strength to clean up will not be there, and the temptation to walk away from each other will be greater. Sometimes, the one who yields develops resentment as they feel that they have been taken advantage of. That person may feel like a time bomb that could explode at any time in the future.

God, when speaking to the Israelites in Isaiah 1:18, said, "Come now, let us reason together" (ESV). When you yield, you deny both of you the opportunity to "reason together" and learn from the situation. Instead of building the relationship, this sets it up for more difficulties. Living at peace with one another does not mean you let go of issues and pretend they are not there. It means confronting the issue, seeking wisdom, and growing together. Your goal as a couple is not to keep peace, but instead to make peace. This takes work.

Withdraw

Sometimes one person will choose to disengage when a conflict comes up. It might look like refusing to talk about the topic, giving the silent treatment, moving into a different physical space, or shutting down emotionally. When one person chooses withdrawal as a weapon to punish the other, the relationship is not only stalled, but the chances of the situation getting worse escalate. Withdrawal gives the impression that the person is not well-invested in the relationship. Withdrawing discourages the one who is willing to work on the relationship, opening the door for them to also give up on the relationship.

If your tactic is to withdraw, know that this also negates the meaning of becoming one. Withdrawing to punish the other person is punishing yourself. You may think you are teaching him or her a lesson, but in the end, your relationship is carrying the weight. Before you know it, the gap of separation grows.

As you prepare to exchange your vows and live them out in your marital home, you will remind each other that the covenant relationship you are getting into is "for better or for worse". When the going gets tough, agree to lock arms and remind each other that you have made a vow to be in this together.

Fighting to win, yielding, or withdrawing from a conflict are temporary plasters that soon wear off and still leave the wound gaping. Choosing to work through a conflict by being intentional in the way you communicate helps heal the wound and grow the relationship.

Our Backgrounds

As with many patterns in our relationships, we are likely to communicate in ways we learned in the homes where we grew up. Being aware of tendencies from our backgrounds will help us weed out some habits we have formed that do not help in effective communication, strengthen the habits that help our communication, and foster openness to learning new ways that we were not exposed to.

When Chao and I (James) first got married, the house sometimes felt like a courtroom where arguments were made and judgements passed. I grew up in a home where communication was mostly one way. My father would say, "Do what I tell you to do and you will not get in trouble." We did not have an environment where emotions were openly expressed. We rarely sat and discussed issues as a family. Rather, my parents discussed the issues and told us what needed to happen.

When I got married, I continued with the same trend. I was not confrontational, but I did not nurture an environment that encouraged open communication. If Chao did something I did not like, I did not bring it up. I just hoped it would go away. I expected that if Chao did not like something I did or said, she needed to work through it on her own and move on. I did not know that unspoken words are like seeds – even when you bury them, they still grow.

On the other hand, I (Chao) grew up in a family that was more emotional and encouraged everyone to express themselves. It was common practice for my family to sit and discuss issues. My mother was sick most of our growing up, and so we learned to team up with our father to help raise the younger siblings. For that to happen effectively, there needed to be open communication.

In our marriage, every time we needed to discuss an issue, I was busy chasing James to get him to talk and he was busy running away from me. When I got tired of chasing him, I would drive to the nearest bookshop and busy myself with reading. James would retreat to a corner in the house to play his guitar. In the evening, we would come back together and move on like nothing had happened.

Slowly but surely, we began to experience the consequences of not communicating effectively. Instead of growing closer together, we were beginning to grow apart. Instead of building unity, we were building a wall. We realized we needed help to learn how to communicate more effectively.

How Should You Communicate to Resolve Conflicts?

Fortunately, the Bible offers counsel for how to communicate. We are to be intentional about our speaking. In Ephesians 4:29, Paul instructs his readers, "Do not let any unwholesome talk come out of your mouths, but only what is helpful for building others up according to their needs, that it may benefit those who listen." Paul points out the need to think through what we are about to say – whether or not we need to say it, how we need to say it, and when we should say it. The goal for our communication is to build and benefit both the one speaking and the one who hears.

We are also to be intentional about our listening. Proverbs 18:13 says, "If one gives an answer before he hears, it is his folly and shame." In moments of anger, we are more apt to ignore what is being said to us and speak whatever comes to our minds. Being discerning and patient to hear the other person before we respond is an art that takes both intentionality in communication and also the power of God through the Holy Spirit. When the one speaking takes the time to think through what they are about to say and the one listening takes the time to listen to what is being said, communication becomes intentional, motivates growth, and benefits the relationship.

Effective and intentional communication helps minimize or even stop a conflict before it starts. When you begin to feel the frustration and discomfort that something is not going well, you can prevent the conflict from escalating by following the pattern of intentional communication below.

Preparing to Communicate

Intentional communication begins before you confront the issue.

Pray Individually

First, pray individually. Going before God as an individual communicates surrender to God's will and power. It shows your need for help from the one who is greater, wiser, and more knowledgeable than you or anyone else. In your prayer, you can search your heart and examine how the conflict has affected you, what your contribution to the conflict is, and if your intention to confront is to pursue oneness in your relationship. The psalmist in Psalm 139:23-24 said, "Search me, God, and know my heart; test me and know my anxious thoughts. See if there is any offensive way in me, and lead me in the way everlasting." An attitude of vulnerability in prayer prepares you to pursue unity in your relationship.

Timing

Timing is important in resolving conflict and in overall improvement of communication in your relationship. For example, if you want to talk about something sensitive, bringing it up while you are driving may not be the best idea. The driver's attention is divided. If the subject is not going well, it may affect the driver's ability to make sound judgements on the road. It may also not be a good idea to bring up sensitive issues during meals. It is important you enjoy your meal. It is also not a good idea to bring up sensitive conversations while you are in the company of others. Sometimes it may feel like the right time to corner the other person and "make" them answer is when there is pressure around. But this may make things worse because they may feel they were being set up, they may feel disrespected, and they may feel you are not sensitive to them.

Consider the time you need to confront the issue in your relationship. For example, it may not be a good idea to bring up an issue right before you go to bed. It is likely that either or both of you are tired, and you may not give it the time and effort that it deserves. Be sure to make enough time to confront the issue. Anything that may cause tension is better left for times when everything is settled, and you can pay attention to each other. The best time to talk is when you agree to talk. Allocate a time and place to sit and have the conversation.

Identify the Real Issue

Sometimes the issue you fight about is not really the main issue; it is a symptom of the main issue. For instance, perhaps Karembo was not primarily upset about Jabali's proposed solution to their temporary need for housing, but the fact that he announced the decision without consulting her first. Another example could be that you are upset that she arrives late without telling you she was held up. You could begin fighting about her timekeeping, but it could be the real issue is that you were worried for her safety. In this case, instead of saying the first thing that comes to mind, think carefully about what is really upsetting you. This way when you choose to say something, you are sure you say what you mean.

Communicating about the Issue

How you communicate through conflict makes all the difference. Communication includes the words that we speak, the gestures we show, and the tone we use. In the midst of a conflict, we often say and do things without thinking, expressing our feelings with strong words and actions. While this way of communicating helps us to speak out instead of bottling it all in, it often does not help heal a relationship or resolve an impending conflict. Here are some suggestions for how to communicate better in a conflict:

Avoid Generalizations

In the heat of an argument, it is not unusual for one or both people to generalize the situation: she "always" raises her voice when talking to you; he will "never" change; she is lazy; or he is rude. This is not the time to bring up everything else that has upset you in the past. Such generalizations often make the situation worse. If you take time to think through such statements before you make them, you will realize they carry unnecessary exaggerations. For example, Karembo said Jabali "never" listens to her. This initiates conflict, because he is prone to be defensive in his response. It also is unlikely to be a true statement. The issue is probably not that he never listens to her, but more likely that in this particular instance, she is not feeling heard.

Do Not Use Blaming Statements

It is common for couples to point accusing fingers at each other with words to imply that the other person is the reason for the conflict. They might sound like, "If you hadn't ... " or "It's your fault that ... " or "You are just selfish." For instance, Jabali accused Karembo of not appreciating the work he was doing to build them a home. Unfortunately, blaming statements and finger pointing will only widen the drift in your relationship and in your communication. Blaming statements often highlight a defect or character flaw in the other person. This approach confronts the person instead of the issue. Instead, remember that you are thinking differently about an issue. If you focus on the differences you hold about an issue, then you will give more thought and energy to reconciling the differences.

Confront the Issue

When in a conflict, try to confront the issue instead of the person. A statement like "you are always late to pick me up" suggests the issue is the person. But the issue is the lateness, not the person. A better way of confronting the issue is highlighting the behaviour and not the person. You can frame the issue as something you both can work on together. For example, "I would like to talk about how we can work towards keeping time when we agree." This way, there is a sense of teamwork in resolving the issue. With this approach, you become focused on finding a solution to the differences instead of trying to change the other person. It shows that you care about each other and are on the same team. You acknowledge that you have a difference of opinion, but you still share a similar goal, which is to work together and strengthen your relationship.

Non-verbal Communication

Effective communication takes into account the non-verbal cues couples use and how such gestures either help or impede understanding. In Jabali and Karembo's case, unhelpful non-verbal cues included shouting, interrupting, throwing up one's hands, walking away, and slamming the door. Helpful cues included Karembo's initial attempt to move closer and whisper to Jabali. Another important non-verbal cue is making eye contact. This makes sure you are heard and that both of you are paying attention to the issue. It not only shows commitment, it can also help both of you read other non-verbal cues from each other, such as facial expressions and body language.

Resolving Conflict

Seek and Grant Forgiveness

If either person did or said something hurtful, it is important to apologize and forgive. Forgiveness is the responsibility of the one in the wrong to ask for, but it is also the responsibility of the one who was wronged to grant it. Verbally asking and verbally granting forgiveness shows commitment to each other and to resolving the conflict. It is important for the one asking for forgiveness to be specific about why they are asking for forgiveness: "Will you forgive me for not keeping my commitment to pick you on time?" For the one granting forgiveness, it is important that they verbally commit, "Yes, I forgive you for not picking me up on time."

Pray Together

Before you confronted the issue, you prayed separately. After you have verbally forgiven each other, praying together invites God to bring healing and rebuild your relationship.

Rebuild Trust

Rebuilding trust acknowledges that just because you have forgiven does not necessarily mean you have forgotten. It is likely that the one who was wronged may be afraid the offense will occur again. It is important to understand that rebuilding the habit of trust is necessary not only for the one wronged, but also for the one who offended, for the good of your relationship. Rebuilding trust also takes a verbal commitment to another level, by showing repentance.

For example, if the issue has been that you do not keep your commitment to be on time, even after you have asked for forgiveness, the one who has granted you forgiveness may still fear that you will go back to the habit of being late. To show that you are repentant and that you are serious about changing, you will need to prove you have changed by keeping the time you have agreed on. As your intended other watches you make the intentional effort to be on time, she or he will begin to trust you again and believe that you have actually changed.

Baraka and Amina

Baraka and Amina had been meeting with us twice a month for four months. A month before their wedding, they walked into our house without making eye contact with each other. This was not the cheerful and bright couple that we had come to know. The spark was gone, the conversation was in a monotone, and they were both going through the motions.

The room fell silent for a while, then Baraka spoke up: "She knows that my work is demanding. This week was our accounts closing week. I needed to have all the numbers done and submitted to my boss before the end of the week. I was not able to finish by Friday, so I had to go to work on Saturday and stayed until late at night. We had agreed I would go over her parents' house for dinner on Friday night. But of course, I did not make it."

Amina picked up the conversation, "On Friday my mum spent most of her afternoon cooking because she had also invited my aunt and uncle to join us for dinner. I went home early from work to help out in the kitchen. Dinner was served on time and everyone was there, except him." She did not turn her head to look at Baraka. "We waited, carried on with light conversation, and took a few glasses of soda as we waited for him. I called his number, but no one picked up. I felt awkward. My aunt and uncle did not say anything, but the look on their faces told me they were just holding back. He did not even call me to let me know he could not come over! On Saturday I did not hear from him until 9 p.m. When he called, he had the nerve to ask me if we are still going to church together the next day!"

Baraka shifted in his chair and turned his face towards Amina. He tried to reach out to touch her shoulder, but she pulled away. "But I wanted to explain to you what had happened. I did not want to talk about it on the phone," Baraka said.

"So, was I supposed to read your mind? What was I supposed to tell my parents? Who knows the next time I will see my aunt and uncle! All they know is that I am getting married to a person who has no respect for me or for my family." Amina looked at us. "I don't even know why we're talking about this. It is obvious he does not care."

How the Relationship Wins

Getting Baraka and Amina to begin to listen to each other was not easy. They were both emotionally charged. They had both been holding back. Now that they felt safe to speak, they said everything they could think of to say. We gave them uninterrupted time to talk before we contributed to the conversation.

It was important for us to hear both Baraka and Amina affirm their commitment to each other and to their relationship while acknowledging the disappointment, especially that Amina felt towards Baraka. After we let them talk uninterrupted for a while, we started by asking, "Baraka, are you committed to Amina and to the relationship you have with her?" Baraka was quick to say, "Of course I am." We then asked Amina the same question, and she also did not hesitate to say, "I am committed to Baraka and to this relationship." They did not see how they could communicate through their conflict, but they were both willing to work through it.

We separated Baraka and Amina into their own spaces. During that time, we asked them to prepare their hearts to resolve their conflict together. We challenged them to consider that the issue was not about who gets to win in the conversation. It was not about ignoring the problem. It was not about minimizing the conflict. It was about finding ground that would help build each other and build their relationship. We also asked them to prepare their hearts by praying for themselves, for the situation, and for each other.

We then brought Baraka and Amina back together. We built ground rules around their conversation. We required that they take turns talking and not interrupt each other. We asked them to allow their conversation to be guided by the fact that they wanted the relationship to win. We encouraged them to consider the words, gestures, and tone they used with each other. We also reminded them that they were confronting the situation, not attacking each other.

After they heard each other out, we asked them to look each other in the eye and ask each other for forgiveness. They both admitted they had a part to play in getting things to where they were. They admitted they could have done things differently and communicated better with each other. They chose to ask for and grant forgiveness.

Before they finished, we reminded them that since they had discovered an area in their relationship that was bound to come up again and again, they needed to be proactive in dealing with the issues it raised. Baraka needed to keep Amina aware of the cycle of his workload so that they did not plan anything when his company was closing the month. If they planned something, he needed to keep Amina updated and change plans in advance if needed. They both agreed on the need to show that they were working towards changing, in order to reestablish trust where it was compromised. They also agreed that since more than the two of them were affected by the conflict, they needed to communicate with both her parents and aunt and uncle as a unified unit.

We had them finish by praying for themselves and for each other. Then we prayed for them. In the end, they left our house encouraged. No one won the argument. Rather, the relationship won.

Conclusion

While you will not be able to avoid conflict in your marriage, you can start now to learn how to communicate effectively when you are in a disagreement. In the next chapters, we will tackle specific areas of conflict that may arise in your marriage. This chapter provides the foundation for how to discuss these topics together. Using Amina and Baraka's example and the tools we have provided in this chapter, we believe you can learn the skills of intentional communication. It takes practice and time, but it is a habit you will keep building and learning as you prepare for and enter into your marriage.

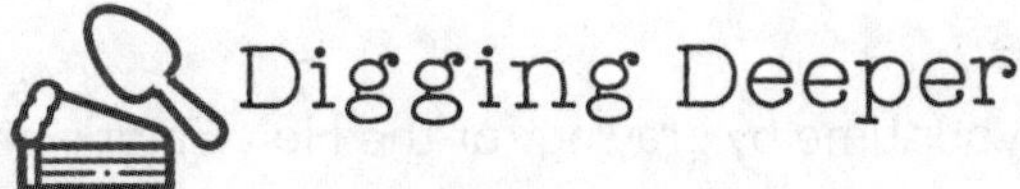

Digging Deeper

Individual Reflection

Find a quiet place with some privacy to complete this section.

1. Think of an area in your relationship that usually results in conflict. It could be finances, your parents, friends, time management, your career, etc.
2. In this specific area of conflict, how do you and your intended other respond? Do you win, yield, withdraw, or communicate intentionally?
3. How do you usually end the conversation on this matter?

Discussion

Meet together and complete this section. Make sure you choose a place where you can talk uninterrupted. Take a few minutes to share about how you saw your parents communicate when you were young. Answer the following questions:

1. What was the best thing you heard your parents say to each other?
2. What was the worst conversation you heard them have with each other?
3. How did your family resolve conflicts when you were growing up?
4. Share with each other how you responded to the individual reflection above.
5. Agree on one conflict you need to resolve together and, using the principles you have learned in this chapter, begin to work through the conflict together.

Prayer

Finish your time by praying for the Holy Spirit's help to communicate intentionally when you are faced with a conflict and for God to give you the strength and commitment to keep growing in this area.

Mentors

What was the conflict you agreed to resolve together?

How far have you come in resolving it? How can your mentors help you continue talking it through? If you have resolved it, debrief how the conversation went.

Take It Further

Affirming communication is important in marriage too!

Write a love letter to each other. Include what you find attractive in the other person and how he or she has helped you grow.

6

Roles and Responsibilities

Karembo and Jabali could not get past their recent disagreement. They agreed to bring it up with their mentors, Krispian and Mishi. "Why don't you come over in the late afternoon, and we can visit over a cup of something hot?" Mishi had suggested.

They made it to their mentors' home before traffic started and helped prepare the hot water and milk. Tea and coffee were always welcome in this cold season. As they sat in the cozy house, slowly sipping their hot drinks, Mishi looked at Karembo. "You did not sound like yourself when you called me. What is going on?"

Karembo began, "Jabali told his builder friend we would be living in his parents' house while I was standing right there. He didn't even think to consult me first!"

Jabali said, "It was my responsibility to come up with a plan. Why can't you see that I was trying to take care of you?"

Krispian said, "We know this is a sensitive issue. We're happy to help you talk through this, but we need you to agree to some guidelines. We want you to focus on the issue and not the person. Also, keep eye contact as you talk." Jabali rubbed his hands together nervously. Karembo frowned.

Mishi added, "Remember, this is one of the many times when you are going to need to agree about roles in your marriage. Agreeing about who makes decisions on what in your marriage will help you keep the unity between the two of you."

Their mentors rearranged the room so that Karembo and Jabali were facing each other. They started with a question: "Jabali, was this the first time you decided something without Karembo's input?"

"No. Karembo did not seem to mind when I made decisions like this before," Jabali responded.

"How about you, Karembo? Have there been times when you have made decisions for the two of you without asking for Jabali's input?"

"Yes, but the decisions I made were different. They were not as weighty as this one," she said.

Krispian said, "So you agree that you individually make some decisions without consulting with each other. The conflict seems to be that you are not in agreement about which decisions you should make only after getting input from each other."

Karembo sat up straight and kept eye contact with Jabali, "I still don't think it was Jabali's role to decide where we will move when we get married."

Jabali replied, "Karembo, I would have failed if I didn't decide. Am I not the man of the house?"

What Are Roles and Responsibilities?

Discussing roles and responsibilities as you go into your marriage gives you clarity about what to expect from each other and how to complement each other in your different roles. It strengthens the oneness you intend to build in your marriage. In this chapter, we will look at the different roles you will play and the responsibilities that come with those roles in your marriage. We will see how culture defines these roles and responsibilities. We will ask how this definition agrees with or contradicts the biblical definition of roles and responsibilities. The chapter challenges you as a couple to understand and agree to live out roles and responsibilities in marriage.

Where Do We Learn about Roles?

When Chao and I (James) got married, we both worked outside of home until we started having children. At home, Chao would be in the kitchen, and I would busy myself with playing my guitar, reading the newspaper, or watching TV. Sometimes I would notice that Chao looked moody, like something was not right. I would not ask, but I would hope that everything was OK with her.

I (Chao) remember coming home tired from work, and James also was tired from work. I would go straight to the kitchen to prepare our meal. I would pick up the laundry I had done before going to work and lay it there in hopes he would fold it. Sometimes I would feel hopeless and helpless as I watched James walk in oblivion. Could he not see that we needed to help each other? Why wasn't he getting the hint?

As we discovered, when we do not talk about our assumptions and expectations, we set ourselves up for misunderstanding. This can lead to heartache, conflict, and confusion between couples.

One of the places we form expectations about roles in our marriages is from our parents or the adults who raised us. We learn from an early age that some roles are specific to males and some are specific to females. Our views may also be influenced by values we pick up from school, peers, the media, and other exposure. We move into marriage and mostly assume we will play similar roles to what we saw modelled to us.

In our marriage, when we talked about our backgrounds, we began to see where each person was coming from.

I (James) grew up with my four brothers and three sisters. On weekend mornings, the girls would help my mother prepare breakfast. My brothers and I would sweep the compound, milk the cows, and get the cows to the field. When breakfast was ready, my sisters would put the food outside for us to eat. Then we would graze the animals and till the land. My sisters would stay home, wash the dishes, clean the inside of the house, and begin to prepare lunch. If we entered the kitchen, it was only to run a quick errand.

Our father worked hard preaching the gospel and building many churches. When he was home, he would wake up and dress up like he was still going out. He would sit under a tree, and we would bring him his food. He received many guests, mostly pastors he discipled. We were not allowed to interrupt him; we would only go where he was when and if he called us. My father never entered the kitchen nor worked alongside my mother in the house. On a regular basis, he prayed with all of us every evening before we went to bed. We would also hear him pray with our mother in their bedroom.

I was picking the cues on how to be the husband in my home. When Chao and I got married, there was no yard to sweep, no cows to milk, and no land to cultivate. But I hadn't considered how that might make my role look different than my home growing up.

I (Chao) grew up with seven sisters and one brother. My mother was sick during most of our growing up. We worked as a team with our father to make sure everyone was taken care of. My father would come home and come straight to the kitchen. He sat and worked with us. We loved to sing with him. In the seasons when our mother was sick, our father cooked for us, and shopped for household items, clothes, and hygiene items.

You can imagine the shock I experienced when I married James, and he seemed not to be working alongside me as our father worked alongside us.

We had a lot to learn about our individual roles and responsibilities to each other. The lessons were not easy, but we were willing to learn – and we continue to learn and build our marriage.

What the Bible Says about Roles and Responsibilities

As you discuss your roles in your upcoming marriage, remember that your first and foremost role is for both male and female to treat each other as equal in value. In Galatians 3:28, Paul tells his readers, "There is neither Jew nor Gentile, neither slave nor free, nor is there male and female, for you are all one in Christ Jesus." After reminding his readers about their trust in Jesus Christ, he tells them that their past attitudes, rooted in inequality between men and women, have been dealt with by the coming of Jesus Christ. While men and women are not the same, they are of equal value before God; that is God's design for them. No one is above the other. As you go into marriage and as you seek to understand and place yourselves in your God-given roles, it is important that both of you understand that first and foremost, you are equal to each other and therefore are deserving of respect and equal treatment.

However, equality does not mean sameness. While men and women are equal, they play different, complementary roles to help build unity in their marriage. Roles are intended to complement each other, not to compete against each other. They build a winning team where everyone takes their position for the good of the entire team. Just as teeth help each other in chewing food when they come together, so is each role essential in your marriage. No role that is more superior than the other. Each role is important to make your marriage whole.

Jabali and Karembo

"What do you mean you are the man of the house?" Karembo responded. The more Jabali tried to explain himself, the worse he made the situation. He looked at Karembo, at their mentors, and back at Karembo. He tried to say something, then sighed and stared on the floor.

Karembo threw both hands in the air and said, "You see, he won't even answer my question!" You could cut the tension with a knife!

"Jabali, do you remember how your parents made decisions when you were growing up?" Krispian asked.

"I grew up with a father who made decisions for my family. I remember when I was young, and we would be home for the school holidays. My father would decide we children needed to visit our grandparents and help out on their farm. My father would decide when we would go and return, how we would go, and what we would do while visiting them. I cannot remember a time when my mother disagreed with him," Jabali said.

"How about you, Karembo?" Mishi asked her.

"My parents called all of us children together to ask our opinion, especially when it was a decision they were about to make that would affect us as a family," Karembo said.

Krispian said, "That should partly explain why you are in this conflict. You are both looking at it based on what you saw modelled in your homes. Why don't you ask each other to explain more about what your families looked like growing up and what those values mean to you now?"

Karembo took a deep breath. "Jabali, what was your parents' marriage like?"

By the time they were done visiting with their mentors, Jabali and Karembo had learned a lot more about each other.

Jabali told Karembo, "I can't promise that I'll never make decisions without you knowing. But I need you to trust that I am doing it for us and because I love you." Jabali told Karembo.

Karembo said, "We can work on creating our own culture as a family and do some things differently from what we saw our parents do." As they left, their mentors were both exhausted and elated.

A Husband's Role

In most of our African homes, the line between what a man does and what a woman does is quite clear. Whether we see it or not, the general assumption is that the opinion of the husband takes precedence and a wife needs to know her place by not arguing when he makes a decision. This kind of traditional arrangement can ensure fewer arguments because everyone knows their place. However, as Jabali and Karembo remind us, this kind of approach does not necessarily build a healthy relationship. Whether you grew up with this kind of belief or not, we encourage you to look at a husband's leadership from the biblical perspective.

Marriage is an institution that has a structure with roles, which give equal worth to both the wife and the husband. As a husband, your role is to lead your wife. In 1 Corinthians 11:3, Paul says, "I want you to realise that the head of every man is Christ, and the head of the woman is man, and the head of Christ is God." Paul gives us the progression of leadership in a home. It begins with Christ being the head of the man. As the man submits himself to the leadership of Christ, he then leads the woman in their marriage. In response, the woman follows the man's leadership. If the man does not take his leadership cues from Christ, he denies himself the authority to lead as God intended for him to. As he hears from Christ about his leadership, he exercises it in his home with his wife. This kind of leadership is not so much about taking charge, decisive measures, or charisma. It is leadership that looks out to serve the other and bring out the best in a relationship.

This type of leadership is best seen when the husband chooses to lead by **loving his wife**. In Ephesians 5:25-28 Paul charges husbands:

> Husbands, love your wives, just as Christ loved the church and gave himself up for her to make her holy, cleansing her by the washing with water through the word, and to present her to himself as a radiant church, without stain or wrinkle or any other blemish, but holy and blameless. In this same way, husbands ought to love their wives as their own bodies. He who loves his wife loves himself.

The husband is to not only love his wife, but he is to love her in spite of herself. Christ loves the church to an extent that he gave himself up for her. Christ did not wait for the church to behave itself, to follow his directives, or even to understand what it means to follow him. While the church is imperfect, he loves it anyway. As you go into marriage as a husband, your responsibility is not to wait until your wife is perfect (she will never be perfect). It is not about how well she will follow your leadership. It is about how you, as a husband, choose to obey Christ and continuously love and nurture her as a gift from God. You choose to love her, not because you are demanding to get something out of her, but because Christ has loved you and he has called you to love her.

One of the ways you can lead her is with tender words of love. Engage her verbally; tell her how much she means to you. A stereotypical African man is portrayed as a strong leader who does not express his emotions, especially in words. Part of the reason we make this stereotype is because we expect the African man to express his love for the lady in a Western manner. We watch movies, interact with our friends from the West, and read novels and conclude that this is how we should love or be loved. If you focus on how much the woman you are about to marry means to you, you will find your own words and actions that express them to her. One of the ways is by asking her how she interprets love, so you can love her the way she would like to be loved. In 1 John 3:18, the writer says, "Let us not love with words or speech but with actions and in truth." Now is a good time to begin to practice leadership in your home by loving her in action and in words.

One of the marks of a leader is to **serve** the one they lead. Mark 10:45 says, "For even the Son of Man did not come to be served, but to serve, and to give his life as a ransom for many." As the leader, see to it that you meet her needs. Where you cannot, team up with her to find help for her. Even as you prepare for your wedding, is there more you can do to serve her? Beginning to sensitize yourself to be ready and willing to serve her prepares you to serve her in your marriage. There will be times when she will come home tired from work, and she will need you to help in the house. When you have children, she will need you to parent alongside her. Sometimes she will need you to just listen to her and not offer solutions, unless she asks. You can begin to serve her now, before you get married.

Part of leading her is **knowing** her. It is difficult, even impossible, to lead someone you do not know well. 1 Peter 3:7 calls on the husband to "be considerate as you live with your [wife]". Part of being considerate to the woman you are marrying is to seek to understand her. Seek to know her fears, cares, disappointments, and joys. Also, pray for her and with her. As a leader, take the initiative to build spiritual nourishment by growing yourself and by helping her grow spiritually. When you pray together, you learn to listen to her, and you also learn to listen to God together. A good leader listens to the one he leads. This also promotes unity in your relationship.

A Wife's Role

As you prepare for marriage, what roles and responsibilities should you prepare for? As you prepare to be a wife, prepare yourself for the important role of being a helper to your intended other. Genesis 2:18 says, "The Lord God said, 'It is not good for the man to be alone. I will make a helper suitable for him.'" God, in the very beginning, established the role of the wife to be a helper to her husband. Now, it is easy to think that a helper is inferior to the one they are called upon to help. But it is serious business when God looks at a man and says, "He can't do it alone; he is going to need help." God then empowers the woman with what it takes to help the man be what God called him to be. This means the married man is empowered the most when his wife comes alongside him as his helper. The word *helper* in Hebrew has the military connotation of an ally. You join forces, act together to fight a common enemy, and protect each other.

You exercise the role of a helper by **respecting** your intended other. You do not wait until you are married to start respecting him. Your effectiveness as a helper is seen in your respect for him. In Ephesians 5:33, Paul charges: "The wife must respect her husband." Notice it is not the husband who is demanding or asking the wife to respect him; it is God, through Paul, who charges the wife to respect the husband. This respect is not demanded of you by your husband, it is a choice you make. Demanding respect is like using your hand to force the sun to set. It is impossible.

One of the ways you can respect your husband is by valuing him in the decisions he makes. Likely there will be times when you disagree with his decisions, but you can still value him as a person and respect the fact that he made a decision about something. You can choose to respect him by being his cheerleader. When you cheer him along as he leads you, you communicate respect to him. Cheering can be seen when you respond in words and deeds that you are for him and not against him, that you stand with him. As you cheer him along, you nurture his self-esteem and affirm his masculinity. He needs to know that you value him as a man and that you value his ideas.

Being a helper to him also means that you choose to **love** him. A wife's love for her husband is the door opening the way for her to help him lead her and grow in his leadership. One way you can show him love as you prepare for your marriage is by supporting him with your gifts, talents, and experiences. For example, perhaps you are good with handling finances. As you prepare for marriage, you could suggest how best to budget for your wedding and offer ideas about how to start saving and investing as you go into your marriage. If you see other ways you can be spending wisely, speak up.

Being a helper to him means that you choose to **submit** to his leadership. Ephesians 5:22-24 says:

> Wives, submit yourselves to your own husbands as you do to the Lord. For the husband is the head of the wife as Christ is the head of the church, his body, of which he is the Saviour. Now as the church submits to Christ, so also wives should submit to their husbands in everything.

In our culture, we have heard of incidences when husbands tried to intimidate or control their wives by demanding their submission. If the wife refused, he might threaten her verbally and, in some cases, use physical violence. There are incidences of wives seeking help from their families, friends, and the church. In some cases, they are encouraged to go back to their married home and continue to submit. There is a big difference between submission and abuse. Right now in your relationship, if you or your intended other believes that a wife's submission means she does whatever her husband says, then we want you to know this is not what we are talking about. We reject this definition.

Also, you may come from a place where the word *submission* is used to infer the inferiority of women. We do not agree with this either. We have established that before God, both male and female are of equal value. No human being is above the other.

Submission is not a role; rather, it is a response to the husband's role. The role of the wife is to be a helper, and one of her responsibilities in that role is to submit to the husband's leadership. The wife's submission is a choice she makes "out of reverence for Christ" (Ephesians 5:21).

The subject of wives submitting to their husbands is only understood and appreciated when viewed in the context of everything else Paul had already said to the Ephesians before he got to the subject of submission. Paul spends the better part of his letter reminding the Ephesians that before Christ, they lived in darkness. Their decisions rivalled God's will for their lives. When Christ came and took them from their darkness into his light, he gave them a new life. It is in this new life where relationships, including marriage relationships, must transform. Because of what Christ has done for them, husbands and wives will be choosing to obey him by submitting to one another out of reverence to Christ. Wives can now submit themselves to their husbands as evidence of their new lives in Christ.

Prince and Sara

Prince and Sara moved to a neighbouring country for their studies, and after graduation, they decided to settle there. Sara landed a good job and thrived. To stay ahead of the competition, she took two years of evening classes, earning an MBA and a managerial position. Prince remembers, "I was proud of Sara and cheered her along. She would be gone some evenings for class. She spent most weekends studying and meeting classmates for group projects. I missed spending time with her, but I knew it was for a season."

Sara says, "At times I felt like giving up, but Prince pushed me to realize my dream."

Meanwhile, Prince had started a business. The money was good and helped cover Sara's tuition. However, as the business grew, his enemies also grew. Competitors wanted to remove him from the market. Former business partners were unhappy that he ended their relationship. His debtors wanted to pay when they felt like it, and some did not want to pay him at all. He sought legal help but didn't succeed.

One day he decided enough was enough. "Sara, I don't know what else to do about my business situation. I am considering whether we should move back home. I know it will be hard for you to start over. I really think in the long run it will benefit us as a family."

Sara said, "The decision sounds rushed to me. Stepping down from my job could mean career suicide. I have already built relationships here, and my friends back home have moved on. I feel tired even thinking about a transition right now."

Prince was tempted to relocate and leave Sara behind. He reflects, "We would not be the first couple to have a commuter marriage, and I could visit her once or twice a month. But I didn't want to be apart. I was at a crossroads."

Prince tried not to push Sara, but it was clear the situation was weighing him down. One Sunday, Sara shared with an older lady from church, "I want to support Prince, but I feel like he is asking too much. I just hope he will look a bit more cheerful."

The older lady listened and made a light comment, "I struggle with what Paul means when he says love doesn't seek its own benefit."

Sara recounts, "One day, I woke up with this strong feeling that I needed to support Prince. He was trying to make the most of his situation, but I could see he was struggling."

Three years later, Prince shared this story with us to show us how much it meant to him that his wife chose to support his decision. They were now beginning to build relationships back home. She ended up changing her career. Even though the new job did not pay as competitively, it supplemented their income. His business sold quickly, and he was able to launch a similar business, this time making wiser business choices. He looked a lot happier.

When we asked Sara what she thought about her decision, she said, "I'm thankful it did not take long before I got a job, but it was not easy. There are things I still miss about our former place. But we are making the most of our lives."

Sara chose to submit to her husband's decision. It was not easy. However, their marriage stood the test and their unity as a couple thrived.

Conclusion

Who will clean the kitchen, who will take care of the bills, or who will lock the door at night are all important subjects to discuss as you prepare for your marriage. Decisions including where you should live, what you should invest in, or how often you should visit your families are also important issues.

However, that is not the place to begin. The husband's first concern is to exercise servant leadership in his home. As he lovingly serves his wife, he responds to his wife's needs with a willingness to listen and work as a team. Then he is not afraid to be found in the kitchen cutting onions as she fixes the stew. He is not afraid to be found changing the baby's diaper as she takes a nap. He is not afraid to make the bed as she takes a shower. He wants to serve her, and because he knows this builds unity in their marriage, he does it wholeheartedly. He is ready and willing to discuss how they should spend their money and where they should invest. He is willing to learn from both their input.

As the wife chooses to be the helper, her concern is no longer focused on why he is not pulling his weight. She listens to his ideas and helps him hone them, encourages him in all aspects of his life, and comes alongside him to make sure bills are paid on time and the house is taken care of. Because she sees and trusts his servant leadership, she is willing to work out conflicts in their relationship, she is willing to wisely correct him, she is willing to forgive and work as a team. She is willing to submit to his leadership because she knows his desire is to build his family as he also serves her. She, therefore, becomes his greatest cheerleader. When he comes home and he feels like a failure, she is quick to remind him of what she has seen him succeed in in the past, to point out his strengths, and to encourage him with a plan to build on those strengths. She is willing to trust God with her husband's leadership in the house.

A couple who chooses to learn and grow in their roles and responsibilities is better prepared to build a strong marriage.

Digging Deeper

Individual Reflection

Find a quiet place with some privacy to complete this section. The aim of this activity is to help you better understand and embrace your role in marriage.

Write your answers to the following:

1. What are some places where you learned about roles for a husband and a wife?
2. How did you see your parents perform their roles in their marriage? For example, who was the leader? Who made the decisions? Who disciplined you as children?
3. What other life experiences have informed the way you view the roles of husband and wife in marriage?

Discussion

Meet together and complete this section. Make sure you choose a place where you can talk freely. The goal for this section is to share with each other your commitment to God's defined roles in marriage.

1. Share your answers to the three questions that you worked on individually.
2. What two new insights have you learned from this chapter?
3. Man: What are three specific ways that your intended other can support you as you prepare yourself for your role to be the leader in your home?

   Lady: What are three specific ways that your intended other can support you as you prepare yourself for your role to be the helper in your home?

Prayer

Thank God for the spouse he has given you. Ask him to help you become a husband or wife who honours God.

Mentors

Share three specific areas of your individual roles in which you agreed to support each other.

Which area do you find difficult? Why? Ask your mentors how they have navigated roles in their relationship. What advice do they have for you?

Take It Further

Enjoy an outing together! You could go hiking, go on a picnic, visit a historical site, or go to your favourite restaurant.

Prayer

[illegible]

Mentors

[illegible]

[illegible]

Take It Further

[illegible]

7

Money in Your Marriage

Having agreed that they would move into Jabali's parents' house adjacent to the main house, Jabali and Karembo started getting it ready. It was self-contained and could be directly accessed through a side gate, without going through the main house. They felt comfortable that they and Jabali's parents could each have some privacy. Karembo agreed that being close to the construction would help them keep an eye on it.

One evening, Karembo stopped by and asked Jabali's mother to accompany her to see the progress at the construction site. "I am so proud of you two, I can't wait to see it!" Jabali's mother said as she put on her gum boots.

The builders were already digging the sewer. Everything else was nearly done, except for the inside doors and the kitchen cabinets. "As soon as there is water and electricity, we will move in and finish the details slowly," Karembo told Jabali's mother.

Jabali's mother returned, and Karembo went back to their new place to take window measurements for the curtains she needed to buy. Jabali said he would stop by later.

It was not long before she heard a commotion outside. "Karembo, would you hold the door for me?"

When Karembo opened it, she saw a big box. By the way Jabali was carrying it, it seemed heavy. She said, "Wow, I can see you are ready to move in. What do we have here?"

Jabali placed the box on one of the two stools in the room that doubled as their dining and living room. "I know we have a few days before we are married and move in. This could not wait. I know you are going to like it! My colleague at work gave me a deal I could not refuse." He talked as he opened the box. "He had ordered a set of these but there was a mistake and he received two sets instead of just one. They are of great quality, and the price is just unbeatable. Could you help me hold the box down as I pull the TV up! You have to see it."

Karembo tried to open her mouth, but nothing come out. She moved in slow motion.

Jabali could hardly contain his excitement. "My friend sold me his speakers as well. But we agreed I could pay him later." Jabali sat down on the other stool and started connecting the wires. "I just need to test it to make sure it will work fine. Since we are yet to put the curtains up, after I am done testing it, I'll put it back in the box and store it at my parents' house." Jabali whistled.

Karembo took three deep breaths and revisited the scene that had just happened. It was only a week ago when they discussed the need to be extra careful with finances going into their marriage, especially over the next three months, to offset their wedding and honeymoon spending. Hadn't they agreed not to make any major purchases until they finished building?

"Really, Jabali? Did you have to do this? Had we not agreed about spending? What is more important, watching your football games on a flat-screen TV or being careful with the little money we have?"

Jabali lightly put his hand on Karembo's shoulder. "Karembo, we will never have enough money. But we can always choose to enjoy life. And you know how even while we have been engaged, we received so many text messages and phone calls from family and friends. They asked us to give towards your aunt who has been sick in hospital for a while. We just gave towards your friend's grandmother's funeral. A week from now my brother's school fees need to be paid. We will always give, give, and give while we also have our own needs. When are we going to spoil ourselves? And don't forget you just bought those bedsheets from your colleague with money we did not have. Now you have to pay slowly for the next three months. You know what, at this rate, I may as well spoil myself."

After this, they both went quiet. They had planned to help each other get the place ready. Jabali finished testing his TV, then packed it up. He mused to himself, "Can't she see how good a deal this is? If I passed it up, there is no telling if we would get another one. Can't she be happy for me? I thought she would be grateful that I want to stay home and watch the games with her instead of with my friends at the bar."

Karembo finished taking window measurements and checked to make sure the kitchen sink was not clogged. She wished she could go home, lock herself in her room, and have a good cry. But they had planned to have dinner with Jabali's parents. It would be rude to cancel. It was going to be a long evening.

Why Is Money Important in Your Marriage?

As you prepare for your marriage, and if you choose to use traditional church wedding vows, part of your vows will include your pledge to hold on to the marriage "for richer, for poorer". You will be entering into a covenant that involves, among other things, the stewardship of money. This chapter discusses why money is important in your marriage, and why beginning to talk about it now will better prepare you to steward it together as a couple. It challenges you as a couple to think about the unity you should have around your money. Your unity regarding money is determined by your understanding that God owns everything, including your money, and that he has given it to you to steward it. Your unity regarding money is also determined by your attitude towards money, and if you are willing to honour God with it. This chapter addresses this unity and common conflicts around finances.

Barriers to Financial Unity

Among couples we counsel, we have noticed several major barriers to financial unity that are so important we believe they must be tackled before you marry. We will discuss them here and guide you on how to move forward.

Separate Bank Accounts

It is not unusual for couples going into marriage to want to keep bank accounts separately rather than sharing finances. For instance, some couples agree that as long as each person is meeting their financial responsibility, they should not give the other person access to their account. There are some couples who have two individual accounts and one joint account that is for day-to-day transactions. Each person knows how much to transfer to the joint account every month, and as long as they keep their commitment, they are not obligated to share how much is in their account and what they are doing with that money. Other couples agree to keep separate accounts and freely allow their spouse to access their accounts.

The first question you need to ask yourselves is why you want separate bank accounts. One reason couples give is because they want their independence. They do not want to feel like they are being controlled. They do not want to be asked too many questions, as long as they meet their financial obligations. Additionally, there could be fears that the other person will mismanage the money. The underlying issue is not necessarily the separate bank accounts but reluctance to depend on and trust each other. If there is a trust issue between the two of you, you have the time to address it now before you get married.

While you will eventually make a decision for your marriage, we encourage you to choose to trust each other and build a strong financial team. Remember, you are preparing to *become one* in every aspect of your lives – and money is one aspect. Having a joint bank account helps you communicate about your financial goals and stay on the same page. Both of you are aware of what you have and how you are spending it. Instead of one person handling their separate account(s), both of you will put your heads together to agree on how to run your bank account(s). In Ecclesiastes 4:9-10a, we read, "Two are better than one, because they have a good return for their labour: if either of them falls down, one can help the other up." As you work together in this area, you get a good return in your finances.

There are some rare situations where having joint accounts may not be possible. For instance, I know of an engaged woman who had opened an account when she was in school overseas. Because of the nature of her work, the account came in handy when she needed to be paid in foreign currencies. She told her future husband about the account, and they agreed to keep it open. They could not add him to the account because he did not have the required documents. Her responsibility, then, was to keep him updated on the account. When they deposited into or withdrew from the account, she documented it on the spreadsheet for all their finances, where he could see it too. This choice maintained their unity and trust.

In most cases, when you choose to have joint accounts, you are communicating something to each other. You are communicating vulnerability, trust, and a willingness to be kept accountable. You show that you are committed to this marriage and to building unity. You are willing to be responsible for your finances and to one another. More so, you are communicating that the two of you have become one. What is "mine" is "yours"; what is "yours" is "mine"; and all of it is "ours".

Family Ties

It is not unusual to hear of a couple who gets married and still depends on their parents for their financial needs. It is also far too common for parents to expect that their children, once they are employed and married, will take up the financial responsibility of supporting them. Whether you are headed towards depending on your parents financially or your parents depending on you, potential conflicts lie in wait.

When you stand before a crowd of witnesses on your wedding day and symbolically agree to "leave and cleave", part of that leaving and cleaving is about finances. You commit to work as a team with your finances and to make your home the first priority. Leaving does not mean you abandon your parents. You can leave your parents, cleave to one another, and still honour them. After all, Exodus 20:12 reminds us of the power of honouring your parents and the promise thereof. Your parents have raised you and, yes, they worked hard to get you to where you are. It was their responsibility to do so. In response, the two of you will need to agree on what honouring your parents will look like in your marriage. Consider your values as a couple and see how they align with your choice to support them. If you are going to support them financially, it should not be because they demand you to do so. You can choose to take care of your parents to the best of your ability while you continue to put your home first.

The Husband's Role

You may be coming from a tradition where only the husband handles the money, and the wife does not question him. If you, the man, have skills and enjoy doing money management, then there is nothing wrong with you and your wife agreeing that you will handle your family finances. Alternatively, if the wife is skilled in money management and enjoys keeping the books, you can decide that she will do it. Regardless who handles the money, it is important that both of you know what is coming in and how it is being spent. Be careful that you do not allow the boss-subordinate mentality – where one of you must keep asking for money to do anything and everything. If you trust each other, even when one of you takes leadership of the financial details, agree that both of you have access to all your accounts. Remember, you are coming into this marriage as one. Therefore, work as one.

Debt

Among newlywed couples we have walked with, the topmost cause for conflict is finances, including debt that was incurred by one or both of them before they got married. Instead of the couple paying attention to each other, they pay attention to bills. Instead of focusing on growing together as a couple, their focus is hijacked by financial survival. An African proverb says, "When the rooster crows, the heart of a debtor skips a beat." Stress around money can lead to communication breakdowns that lead to isolation from each other and a general dissatisfaction in marriage. Such a couple finds out the hard way that while a debt can get mouldy, it never decays.

As you go into marriage, do everything you can to clear your debts so that you can start your lives together free from it. If you are unable to clear any debt amount before you get married, agree on a plan to clear it as soon as possible.

We also encourage you not to borrow to pay for your wedding expenses. While there may be circumstances that only you as a couple can understand, going into debt to pay for your wedding is generally a financial irresponsibility. Plan a wedding that you can afford, however small or simple it may appear. Do not fall into the trap of having a wedding to please others. Remember, after financing the wedding you will need to finance the marriage. And while the wedding lasts for several hours in one day, a marriage is meant to last until death.

In your marriage, agree about how you will stay away from debt. One of the best ways to avoid debt is by agreeing not to spend beyond what you can afford. There are a few exceptions, such as when the expense will bring long-term investment returns and the payments will not become a burden.

In addition to getting out of debt, it is important to discuss how these debts came to being. Are there attitudes towards money that need correcting? You need to learn healthy ways of spending money and how to work with what you can afford. If one of you has a history of bad financial decisions, working through that area as an individual and as a couple will protect you from making decisions that could lead you back to more debt.

Different Core Financial Commitments

It is to be expected that you will have differences around money going into your marriage.

Whatever your differences, before you are married, it is very important that you commit to financial responsibility. You may not resolve your differences before you get married, but we do encourage you agree to a few core values:

- Live within your budget
- Stay out of debt and pay off any existing debts
- Give cheerfully
- Invest for the future

If there is no agreement on this, then it becomes difficult for the two of you to move together. Some of these may require discipline. You may never have made a budget before, or you may just be starting to invest. Thankfully, regardless of your tendencies, financial responsibility is a habit that can be learned. What is essential before you get married is that you are both committed to working together to achieve these goals. Do not give up!

Strengthening Financial Unity

If you are able to resolve the common pitfalls above, you can move into your marriage with greater confidence and trust in each other – an important foundation for healthy financial unity. We also want to provide you with some tools and principles you can use to continue building your financial unity as you begin your life together.

We already discussed the importance of staying out of debt, but let's examine the other three of the four principles in more detail.

Live Within Your Budget

To create a realistic budget, you will need to clarify how much money you, as a couple, have and how much you anticipate you will earn on a regular basis. Having this information will help you develop a more realistic budget.

You will also need to identify the expenses you anticipate in order to compare this with the money you have on hand. To get an accurate understanding of how much you spend, keep a record of all your spending. It helps to save all the receipts of your purchases. There are places such as the market or the neighbourhood kiosk where getting receipts is difficult or impossible. Write down those expenditures. Before the end of the day, log all your expenditures on your expense sheet (a **Sample Budget** is given on pages 189-191). We recommend you do this every day for at least six months. At the end of each month, come together and evaluate. Compare your spending with your income. Look at any trends in your spending habits. Ask what adjustments you may need to make to meet your financial goals. We recommend you start now keeping a record of all your spending in preparation for your wedding. This will help you see where the money is going.

To live within your budget, you will also need to cultivate contentment. It takes a commitment to God, to each other, to your values, and to your financial spending decisions to be content to live within your means. The temptation to discontentment will creep in from different angles, some blatant, some subtle. You will see it on billboards marketing the lie that you can only be happy if you have what they offer. You will face it when you compare your standard of living with your friends'. Contentment is a shared decision to celebrate what you have and adjust your spending in line with your income levels and circumstances. One of the secrets to contentment is to be careful you do not lead your lives to please others but instead focus on pleasing God by spending his money well and being thankful for what he has given you. Trust God for a spirit like Paul's who said in Philippians 4:11-13:

> For I have learned to be content whatever the circumstances. I know what it is to be in need, and I know what it is to have plenty. I have learned the secret of being content in any and every situation, whether well fed or hungry, whether living in plenty or in want. I can do all this through him who gives me strength.

Contentment communicates satisfaction and gratitude to God because you have everything you need. As you prepare to get married, you can begin to be intentional about being content by, for example, by having a wedding that you can afford.

Give Cheerfully

The money God has given you is to bless you and provide for your needs, but he also wants you to use it to give to others, blessing them. We encourage you to discuss where you will give your money. Some areas to consider include:

The church and organizations. Have you agreed on a local church you will attend once you are married? We encourage you to give your regular tithe through your church. You may also seek to understand what the church spends its income on, for example, social justice issues. As you identify a ministry or outreach that is in your passion, choose to give towards that initiative.

In addition to the church, you can choose to give to other organizations that steward their resources and time towards social issues. For example, you can agree to give towards poor people or widows by identifying an organization that you trust, and that works among marginalized people. While you cannot go where these organizations are able to go, you can choose to send those organizations with your regular financial contributions.

Your family. Who in your family do you give to on a regular basis and what one-time needs within your family are you willing to meet? Since you cannot meet all the needs around you, how are you going to make sure you are not exhausted in your giving? If your parents or immediate family members have a regular need (supporting your parents, paying siblings' school fees, etc.), agree on the frequency and the amount.

When you have a budget that specifies what you will give towards your relatives, it helps you work together. While this issue is not easy, starting with agreement between the two of you on what you can support and having a budget line to reflect this is a good beginning.

Friends and the community. Sharing what we have with family and friends is something we grow up with, and our communities encourage this value. It is not unusual for us to be asked or to ask for help to meet wedding or funeral expenses, to pay school fees for relatives, or to contribute towards hospital bills for a family, friend, or church member. Because it is in our culture to come together to raise funds for different needs, it is important to anticipate this. Work together as a couple – agree on criteria for giving towards these initiatives and agree on how much to give when that need arises. While you cannot give towards every need represented in your circle of friends and community, your involvement with others is foundational in building and maintaining relationships. These are the same people who have and will come alongside you when there is need, not only in your home as a married couple, but also in your family circles.

Invest for the Future

Godly wisdom includes saving for the future. Luke 14:28 says, "Suppose one of you wants to build a tower. Won't you first sit down and estimate the cost to see if you have enough money to complete it?" As you go into marriage, make financial goals together.

As stewards of God's money, you should agree as a couple to put aside money for your future, including the increased needs when you start having children. The Living Bible Translation in Proverbs 21:5 says, "Steady plodding brings prosperity; hasty speculation brings poverty." Proverbs 21:20 also states "The wise store up choice food and olive oil, but fools gulp theirs down." As you start your life together, begin slowly and steadily to save. You are not on a competition with anyone. Save according to the budget you have agreed on and keep adjusting the amount as you evaluate your expenses and needs. Right now, it may feel impossible to save because of all your wedding preparations. Start small and build up as you go. Just keep it up!

Communicating about Money

Every marriage will include conflicts around money. Do not be afraid of conflicts; what is important is that you learn how to resolve them. For instance, you may find that one of you is cautious about spending, while the other spends more easily. If you are the careful one, chances are that you have built certain disciplines, but you may also feel fear and anxiety around money. If you are a spendthrift, chances are that you enjoy money, but your lack of a budget could indicate that you have not affirmed who really owns your money. Talking through your habits can help you realize when one of you may need to loosen up and allow yourself to enjoy the money God has given you and the other would need to be more disciplined with the money God has entrusted to you. The beauty of marriage is that two independent people come together, not so one person depends only on the other, but so they both depend on each other in interdependence, and on God. Here are some principles that can help you communicate about money in ways that build your financial unity:

1. **Be willing to listen.** Instead of pointing fingers at each other, be intentional in listening to each other. As you listen, work hard not to make preconceived conclusions. Just because you know it a certain way does not mean yours is the only way things are done. The goal is unity, not division. You want to respect each other even when you do not agree. Don't lose sight of the love you share for each other.
2. **Be willing to confront.** Be honest with each other. You must take the risk, otherwise the clarity that you need to communicate with will be compromised. If you think you are the only ones having trouble discussing difficult issues, remember that many people have gone through this before you, and you will not be the last ones. Even Ecclesiastes 1:9 says, "What has been will be again, what has been done will be done again; there is nothing new under the sun." Confront the issue and keep at it. The worst thing that can happen is usually the result of not confronting the issue. When you come to the place and time to talk finances, remember to be honest with each other. Your marriage should be built on the foundation of honesty. If you are not honest with each other, it will be impossible to work effectively as a team.
3. **Prepare.** The money subject is already a sensitive and emotional issue. It can evoke emotions you never thought you had. As much as you possibly can, prepare each other by agreeing on the time and place to discuss finances. Often when you want to talk about money in the moment, you have not thought it through, and you are likely to react instead of being proactive. Ecclesiastes 3:1, 7b says, "There is a time for everything, and a season for every activity under the heavens . . . a time to be silent and a time to speak." Learn to pace yourself and bring things up when you need to, not when you want to.

4. **Consider your background.** As you talk about money, be aware of what you carry with you. You are carrying years of habits that have formed as you have watched your family interact around money. Your exposure, experiences, and even temperaments may impact how you handle money. Remember that the other person also comes with their own background as well. Sometimes, even if you both think the same way, that does not make it right. The measure of your values is the Bible. Anything that runs contrary to the Bible, even when you both agree about it, should be abandoned as you build unity as a couple. Seek counsel from God and from those you trust.
5. **Keep practicing.** Remember, practice makes habit. Even when you start and you disagree, at least you have started talking. Do not despise those messy beginnings. You always start from somewhere. Persistence is the key. One of the ways to create a habit of healthy discussions about money is by making special dates to go and discuss your money status. Talk about the good, the bad, and the ugly. As you build this habit, you will not need to wait until there is a crisis for you to discuss money. It will already be built into your regular conversations.
6. **Pray.** Don't underestimate the power of prayer. Remember the words of Jesus in Matthew 18:19-20: "Truly I tell you that if two of you on earth agree about anything they ask for, it will be done for them by my Father in heaven. For where two or three gather in my name, there am I with them." Prayer is powerful, and where two agree in prayer, the power is multiplied.

Conclusion

As you prepare for your marriage, you will have a lot more questions than answers. Remember, like any journey, there is always a place of beginning. Even if this is not your first marriage, you are still beginning with the one you are getting married to. Go into marriage well equipped to work through financial issues, and remember that disciplines are formed with practice. Right now, you may need to focus more on day-to-day financial needs. You may be overwhelmed as you learn each other and put money where it belongs. Start working on your budget, and commit to staying on it, even when you do not feel like it.

A time will come when things will begin to make sense. Your spending habits will emerge. You will get better at resolving the different money conflicts you will have. As you learn each other and your spending habits, you will develop a vision for your money in the future. The truth that God owns everything is not something you learn to apply quickly. It is a practice you keep working on. As you move from "my money" to "our money", you will find your stride in managing money as a team. You will learn to manage money out of reverence to God, recognizing him as the rightful owner of what you have. God owns everything.

Jabali and Karembo

Jabali's parents were wonderful hosts. Dinner with them helped ease the tension. His mother said, "The construction is going really well. I enjoyed being out there with Karembo to see what they have done so far."

"Thanks, Mum."

"I like what you are doing with your little place, Karembo. It sounds like you will have the curtains up in just a few days."

Jabali's dad chimed in, "Sounds like you kids are ready for the World Cup. With a flat-screen TV like the one I see in that box, it seems to me that all you need is to close those curtains, get some popcorn, and enjoy the games."

His mother chimed in, “Don’t dream too far ahead, they don’t have water or electricity yet.”

“True. That’s the problem with building, it always takes longer and costs more than you expect. Remember when we built this house, Jabali? You were so excited the day you got your bedroom door.”

Jabali did remember. He used to feel annoyed that he could hear everything through the curtain in his door frame. Now that he was older, he realized his parents had been tight on money. When the end of the month approached, he would overhear his parents arguing about bills. He didn’t want to start his marriage fighting over money.

“That’s a good reminder, Mum. Karembo and I said we would try to save money when we decided to build. Maybe buying that TV was jumping a bit too far ahead.”

Jabali’s father was about to respond, but his wife gave him a gentle shoulder squeeze. He chuckled instead. Jabali helped his mother clear the table. As they walked into the kitchen to get the tea tray ready, his mother whispered, “Wisely said. I am proud of you, son.”

As Jabali dropped Karembo off at her home, he said, “You’re right, Karembo. I should not have bought that TV without your input, especially when we had already agreed we need to be careful with money. Let’s try to return it.”

“Thank you, Jabali. And I have no problem with us getting a nice TV when the time comes! We are just beginning our marriage. We will have many opportunities to buy an even nicer TV.”

“Seeing my parents reminded me that I don’t want us to start our marriage worrying and arguing about money.”

“Me neither. Maybe it would help if we worked out a budget so we can plan together how to spend our finances.”

Digging Deeper

Instead of an individual reflection, this chapter has a longer discussion section to work through together. Make sure you choose a place where you can talk uninterrupted.

Prayer

Begin this exercise by praying together. Pray especially that you will be united in the decisions you make about your finances.

Discussion

You will find a suggested **Sample Wedding Budget** in the Activities and Resources section on pages 187-188.

1. Use it to begin to practice how to set a budget together. Your wedding budget may not include every suggested item and in some cases, your budget will have more items. If you have a wedding committee, you might need to consult with them to make sure the line items for which you are raising funds are estimated at the price your committee has also estimated.
2. Using similar budgeting principles from the **Sample Wedding Budget**, create your honeymoon budget.
3. End your time together by reading Psalm 24:1: "The earth is the Lord's and the fullness thereof, the world and those who dwell therein." This helps you remember that everything, including your money, belongs to God.

Prayer

Close by thanking God for the finances he has given you and asking him to guide you as you make these budgets.

Mentors

Moving on from the Wedding Budget, begin to consider your everyday finances in your marriage.

Use the **Sample Budget** on pages 189-191 to discuss income and expenses. Take advantage of your time with your mentors to work through this together. Can they help and advise you in preparing a draft budget?

Take It Further

Cook your favourite meal and share its importance.

8

Sexual Intimacy

"How was your afternoon with the ladies yesterday?" Jabali asked Karembo. They were on their way to see the pastor who was to officiate their wedding in only seven days. The day before, Karembo had had a bridal shower, and Jabali spent the evening eating goat meat with the boys.

Karembo giggled, then laughed out loud. "Why are you asking me about my afternoon? How did it go with the big boys you were with last night? I tried to call you once to remind you that pastor had asked if we could move the appointment forward by 30 minutes, but you were nowhere to be found."

Jabali loved it when Karembo was in a playful mood, letting go and sharing a hearty laugh. "But Karembo, I asked you first. Why do I feel like you are avoiding my question?" he said with a grin.

Jabali was right. Karembo was still trying to wrap her mind around everything that had happened at her bridal shower. She knew all the ladies there quite well. Even her friend, Malkia, travelled from out of town to celebrate her on this big night. *I thank God my mum was not there*, she thought to herself. Her three aunties and their friends somehow managed to sneak into the event. She loved them dearly, but she wasn't sure if she was ready for the "girl talk" they seemed excited to be a part of. After everyone introduced themselves and served up refreshments, the younger aunt called everyone to attention.

She asked them to move to the next room, where Karembo's friends, led by Malkia, had changed into "interesting" outfits. They seemed to cover what Karembo saw as only the sacred places. They serenaded her with an upbeat song and had her join them in the dance. The ululations were deafening: *lililililililiiii!* The older women waved any piece of cloth they could find. The younger ladies embraced, and everyone joined in another song.

Karembo's aunt had to turn off the music to get the ladies to settle. They pulled Karembo to a comfortable seat in the middle of the room. She knew there was a growing trend to invite sex experts to bridal showers for some lessons, and she was starting to get nervous. She tried to make light conversation. "Wait until it is your turn," she told one of the young single ladies. "Malkia, please try not to embarrass me!"

Her older aunt, who had been sitting quietly, called out to one of the ladies, "Bring me that piece of cloth. Give me that bag with my tools. Girls, be quiet as I give instructions." She walked over to Karembo and said with a wink, "You, come and kneel right here." The older ladies surrounded Karembo, while the younger ladies watched and giggled.

Karembo's thoughts were interrupted by Jabali. "We did the *men thing*, you know. We had a lot of fun." One of his friends started the rest of the boys off with a song that is usually sung when warriors come home after a victory. They all stood, stomped, clapped, and shouted until the place felt like it was shaking. "Aside from eating a lot of goat meat, there is not much to say." Jabali laughed to himself, thinking of how his friend had told him, "You'll do just fine. You know how to ride a bicycle. This is like that. Just remember, practice makes perfect." Jabali dared not say anything, and instead joined the roar of laughter. Where the conversation had gone from there … he wasn't sure how to bring that up with Karembo.

They were now at the church compound. Jabali looked at Karembo, and Karembo gave him a knowing look. They laughed as they held hands and walked towards the pastor's office.

Talking about Sex

In our cultures, we are often discouraged from talking about sex – perhaps until the bridal shower gives us a chance to lighten up and discuss it. If the subject comes up, it is probably to remind us how terrible it is to engage in sex outside of marriage. We agree that premarital sex is a destructive sin that affects your relationship with God, with yourself, and can affect your relationship in marriage. But if God himself was not ashamed to talk about sex, we should not be ashamed to talk about it either!

In this chapter, we will discuss the importance of sex in your marriage and God's design for sex. We encourage you to look forward to sharing your sex lives with each other and help you to prepare for this union. We also give you the opportunity to consider any fears, expectations, and issues about sex as you prepare for marriage.

Expectations around Sex

We already dedicated a chapter to discuss the subject of expectations. Whether you have been involved in premarital sex or not, the two of you are going into your marriage bed with expectations, many of which are unspoken. Beginning to discuss your expectations before you get married will open the door for further conversations once you get into your marriage. We aren't recommending that the two of you dwell on the subject of sex, lest you are tempted to be intimate early, but it is important that you begin a conversation now that gives you a point of reference when you go into your marriage.

For example, one of you may be thinking that sex will be happening every day while the other assumes it will happen only on weekends. One of you might want the room to be dark to help create the mood, and the other is looking forward to shining the room with the brightest bulb they can find in the market! One of you might think sex should only take place in your marriage bed, while the other cannot wait to have the experience in different parts of your house. And while one of you might expect sex should only happen at night when you are going to bed, your intended other might be thinking you both can run home during your lunch breaks and include sex on your lunch menu! Whatever expectations you might have, talking about them now will help better prepare you for each other.

It is helpful to be aware of where you formed these expectations. We learn about sex from different "schools". These include social media platforms (television, internet, radio, billboards), parents and other relatives, the schools we attend, sexual experimentation, comments from peers, and sometimes content from church. These "schools" influence our understanding of and attitude towards sex. When we get married, they can potentially influence our response to sex. It is helpful to be aware of what these are and how they may influence your relationship.

Ebenezer and Peace

Ebenezer and Peace wished they had talked about these influences before they got married.

I ran into Peace while I was out shopping. She had been back from her honeymoon for a month. The wedding day had been full of activity, and I hadn't had the chance to give her a congratulatory hug. I was elated to see her, but I noticed her tired eyes. "Do you have time for a quick cup of coffee?" I asked. We found a table at a corner, and I asked, "You look tired. Are you back at work already?"

"No, I have another two weeks before I report to my new position," she said. She lowered her voice and moved closer to me. "Things are not going that well in bed. It's been really hard. I just feel uncomfortable. Ebenezer has tried to help me. He wants to talk about it, but I don't know how to have that conversation. He is getting frustrated. We are newlyweds, and we are already having problems!" Peace could not hold back her tears.

Our quick coffee time lasted over an hour, and it was worth it. "I cannot begin to tell you how relieved I am to have someone to talk to," Peace said. I invited her and Ebenezer to our home to discuss the subject as couples.

A week later, Ebenezer shared his side of the story. "Our problem started on the first night of our honeymoon. I tried to touch Peace and she cringed. I asked her if anything was the problem, but she has not told me what the issue is. I feel like Peace is not there with me."

Peace was quiet for a while and avoided looking at Ebenezer.

"Peace, would you like to respond?" I asked.

Finally, Peace opened up. "My mother always told me sex before marriage was a terrible sin. She made me feel that even looking at a boy was sinful! I spent my youth running away from boys. When Ebenezer and I started dating, I was so thankful that he respected himself and me enough to wait for marriage."

She shared that when they were preparing for marriage, they did not talk about sex. "We assumed that once we got married, it would be a natural thing to talk about." What Peace learned quickly was that after the wedding, her mind did not automatically switch from seeing sex as sinful to seeing it as beautiful and pleasurable. "I want to enjoy sex in my marriage, I just don't know how," she said.

Why God Gave Us Sex

Many of the messages we receive about sex from our various "schools" are misleading and can set us up for frustration and disappointment. As Christians, it is important to ground ourselves in the truth of what the Creator of sex has to say.

God created sex for pleasure. This pleasure is not just for one person, but for both the man and the woman. We have mentioned how the man and woman become "one flesh" in marriage (Genesis 2:24). This bond of one flesh includes the pleasure of sexual intimacy in marriage. As you begin your marriage, remember that God has given sex for you to enjoy with your spouse! In 1 Corinthians 7:4 Paul says, "The wife does not have authority over her own body but yields it to her husband. In the same way, the husband does not have authority over his own body but yields it to his wife." In marriage, your bodies will belong to each other. You are to take care of and find pleasure in what belongs to you.

Sex in marriage also helps solidify the emotional bond of friendship with your spouse. In Song of Solomon, the bride says of her groom, "This is my beloved, this is my friend" (5:16b). When you, as a husband, are sexually fulfilled, you feel more confident, and your masculinity is affirmed. Knowing that you make your wife happy and that she is interested in you gives you strength. A sexually fulfilled man nurtures an environment where he is more responsible both at home and outside of home. He is emotionally satisfied, so he feels empowered to act in his married life and more determined to conquer in other areas of his life.

When you, as a wife, are sexually fulfilled, you feel appreciated and your femininity is affirmed. A sexually satisfied woman is emotionally healthy. She knows she is not just a tool to entertain the man and have him prove something; rather, she and her husband have a shared, healthy, and powerful emotional bond.

Sex in marriage helps to protect your marriage. Writing to the church in Corinth about marriage, Paul said it was good to remain unmarried. But for people who could not control their sexual passions, Paul advised them to get married. Paul also talked to those who were already married and urged them not to deprive each other of sexual intimacy, so as to protect each other from temptations from Satan (1 Corinthians 7:1–9). Regular married sex helps both the man and the woman stay pure and faithful to each other. It serves a powerful function of protecting you from temptations to seek sexual fulfilment outside of marriage.

Sex in marriage is also intended for the two of you to have children. In an earlier chapter, we mentioned that one of God's purposes for marriage is passing a godly legacy on to your children. The choice not to have children and focus on other areas, such as a career, is becoming more and more common. But in Genesis 1:28, after God had blessed husband and wife, he clearly called them to "be fruitful and increase in number." Another one of God's purposes for sex is to procreate.

We recognize that you might choose to use birth control. It can help you plan when you will start having children and space out your pregnancies. We will discuss birth control later in the chapter in more detail. Whichever birth control method you choose, we encourage you to still have children because it is one of God's purposes for sex in marriage.

We also recognize that some couples may not be able to have children for different reasons. Children are a gift from God. Should you go into marriage and try to have children, only to find it challenging, we encourage you to seek help. Ask your mentors for guidance and other sources. Talk to your doctors and follow the guidance they give you. Remember to pray. God can do what seems impossible with humans. We read in the Bible about God blessing the fruit of women's wombs and intervening for barren women to show that he intends for children to be born in a married home.

Sexual Struggles

Sex is beautifully designed by God, and he wants you to find pleasure in it in your marriage. However, sometimes our minds can agree with this, but our hearts do not. Do you carry negative attitudes towards sex? Are you uncomfortable or embarrassed to talk about sex? When you think about sex, are you looking forward to sharing those moments with your intended other? Or is there pain, fear, or shame in your heart?

Some people, like Peace, may associate sex with sin and be very uncomfortable around sex. For other people, your own sexual sin or a sexual sin committed against you could be influencing your attitude towards sex. You may feel guilty about sexual involvement in your past. You may struggle with addictions, including pornography or masturbation. Any kind of sexual addiction can lead to guilt, shame, unforgiveness of self, and fear that you can never overcome the addiction. You may have experienced sexual abuse in the past. This can also lead to fear, shame, unforgiveness, and a negative attitude towards sex. Whichever experience you might have, this is the right place and the right time to confront any addiction, correct any negative attitude, or seek healing from any abuse. We desire you to begin your marriage encouraged and more ready to enjoy God's gift of sex in marriage.

Sexual Sin and Addiction

If you are struggling with the sin of sexual addiction, begin by acknowledging that you have an addiction and that it is a problem. Refusing to acknowledge that you have a problem does not make the problem go away. When not dealt with, sexual addiction can turn into a vicious cycle where you try to quit, only to find yourself back in it. This can make you give in and give up.

When you acknowledge you have a problem, you open the door to look for a solution. Now go before God and ask for his forgiveness. There is nothing he cannot forgive. This is the beginning of moving towards your healing. By asking for forgiveness, you not only take responsibility for your sin, you also invite God to come forgive you and be the solution to your problem. Here is a sample prayer you can pray from your heart:

> Jesus, I admit that I have been involved in [name the addiction]. I admit that this is sin against you and against my body that is your temple. I come to you and ask for your forgiveness. I ask you, by the power of your Holy Spirit, to help me not to turn back to this addiction. I present my body to you for your service. From now on, I choose to keep my sexuality for marriage only. Even when Satan tries to overwhelm me with the temptation to go back to this addiction, through fear, shame, guilt, or anxiety, I will choose to believe the truth that you have forgiven me and you have restored me. I thank you, Lord, for forgiving me and for giving me a new beginning. I thank you that you have accepted me. I now choose to also accept my body and agree with you that it is clean and pure before you.
>
> In Jesus's name, Amen.

Whether for addiction or the act of engaging in sex before marriage, sometimes the person we have the hardest time forgiving is ourselves. Forgiving yourself simply means that you are accepting God's forgiveness and refusing to be bound by guilt, shame, or even the cycle of going back and forth. It can be helpful to verbalize that you have forgiven yourself. Here is a sample prayer: "In the name of Jesus, I choose to forgive myself for [mention the sexual sin or addiction], and I choose to no longer walk in guilt and shame." Remember that the addiction does not define you; you are no longer bound by it.

These prayers are not quick fixes. Addictions do not happen overnight. They are habits we pick up over a period of time. Many times, they are subtle in how they present themselves. So, you will need to choose to do what James 4:7 says: "Submit yourselves, then, to God. Resist the devil, and he will flee from you." Resisting means you choose to walk away from habits or activities that will tempt you to sexual sin. Such habits include looking at pornographic material, being in the company of those who encourage the habit, going to places that would encourage the temptation, or being isolated from those who know you and can keep you accountable.

When you are tempted to fall back into sin or to feel the guilt and shame, God equips you to fight with his Word. Pick up the Word of God as your weapon of choice. Read and recite its truth to train your mind in new ways of thinking and habits. Study it with others to learn who God is and what he says about you.

Another way to submit and resist is by being accountable to someone. This can be your intended other or your mentor. Your local church may also be resourceful in helping you stay away from the addiction and help build you up. Your healing will depend on your willingness to be helped and your choice to be vulnerable as you get the help you need.

Even if you have relapses, which can happen, find your footing and keep working on it. If habits do not happen overnight, healing from them can also take time. It is like nursing a nasty wound. You keep dressing and applying medication on it. You undress the wound and apply the medication again until the wound heals. After it heals, you look at the scar. You remember how far you have come, the process it took to heal, and how much you do not want to be in that situation again. But when you involve God in your journey, you can have confident hope that healing is on its way.

Sexual Abuse

If you were sexually abused, you might not be looking forward to sex in your marriage. It makes sense that there is a contradiction between what we are telling you – that sex is beautiful and was created by God – and the fact that it was used by someone as a weapon to harm you. We would not want to take lightly how you feel. We come alongside you to encourage you to know that nothing is too difficult with God. The Bible calls God the God of restoration. Psalm 71:20-21 says, "You will restore my life again; from the depths of the earth you will again bring me up. You will increase my honour and comfort me once more." God is able to heal your pain.

The process of restoration is a journey. Usually it includes seeking help from a counsellor or a mentor who will walk the journey with you. The process could take several months, and even when you have gone through counselling, you may have moments when the pain of the abuse seems overwhelming. Even in those moments, do not give up.

Part of the restoration process will be learning that it is not your fault that you were sexually abused. Restoration will also involve you choosing to forgive the person who sexually abused you. Forgiveness does not mean you are tolerating the sin, it does not mean you can completely forget, but it means you are no longer bound by the abuse that was done to you. You forgive them not because you want to let them off the hook, but because you do not want to stay hooked to bitterness. That person gets to pay the consequences – now or in eternity – in ways you may never find out. But you can choose to walk free from bitterness about what was done to you.

Do not fight it alone. Your intended other can help you pray and keep you accountable to stay in your resolve. Your mentors are a good place to go to talk through the process of healing. Your church is also a good place to find resources to help you walk free from the consequences of sexual abuse. We have included some resources for further help on sexual abuse and sexual addiction on pages 138-140.

Mimi and Kwame

Mimi shared her story with me. "I did not think my past would come back to haunt me on my wedding night. At the back of my mind, I still had this nauseating feeling about what was done to me by my uncle when I was young. But I felt that my love for my husband would overcome those feelings, and I would enjoy sex. I was wrong." At their honeymoon, she said, "All systems locked. I tensed up when he touched me. I felt it was something dirty. I could not tell him anything other than that I couldn't do it."

Her husband, Kwame, said, "We came back from our honeymoon a very miserable couple. One of the hardest parts for me was that I did not know about the sexual abuse she had suffered until after we were married."

Fortunately, Mimi and Kwame looked for help. They found a couple who had counselling backgrounds. "It was not easy, but we are so glad we did it."

It helped Mimi to be affirmed. "I was just thankful to be reminded that it was not my fault that I was sexually abused. It helped to know that how I felt was something a sexually abused person goes through. I was so thankful it was not a secret I carried alone, but that Kwame knew, and he was on board to help both of us heal."

As they moved on in their marriage, they knew that even if those feelings of shame, pain, anger, and guilt returned sometimes to Mimi, they had access to God their helper and to people they could turn to for help.

Mimi said with a laugh, "We take it one day at a time. On a scale of one to ten of enjoying our sex life, I would say we are about to pass six!"

Preparing for a Fulfilled Sex Life

There is a popular but mistaken view today that getting married is like buying a car, so one should "test the equipment before you take it home." But someone else's body is not a machine, and sex is not merely about proper physical functioning of moving parts for one's own immediate pleasure. Sex in marriage is a form of communication that requires you each to choose to give of yourselves and to fulfil each other.

Sex is not only physical; it also engages your spirit, mind, emotions, and will. Instead of testing "the equipment", you should prepare for marriage by building habits and disciplines that will strengthen your sexual intimacy as a couple. These habits include preparing your spirit, mind, emotions, and your will.

You may have committed to wait until marriage before engaging in sex. In some circles, you may feel awkward, as if you are the only ones. You are doing the right thing to wait. Soon you will be married and have all the time you need to explore sex together and grow together in your sex life.

We want to remind you, though, that you will still need to make the ongoing choice to guard yourselves against the temptation to engage in sex outside marriage, even after you are married. Before marriage, you choose not to engage in sex. After marriage, you choose to engage in sex only with your spouse. In both cases, you will need to avoid any hint of sexual sin, such as viewing videos or pictures that invite sexual thoughts, engaging in pornography, or entertaining any other sexual addiction.

You can continue to build your self-control and love for your spouse now by avoiding any hint of sexual sin. Even if you aren't touching each other, you may be indulging in phone sex with each other or discussing sex with the intent to put pressure on the other person. What you choose to look at and talk about affects your thoughts and can lead to the act of sex. If you are unsure, ask yourself some clarifying questions: Does what I am looking at, talking about, or doing build God-intended intimacy between the two of us?

You will also need to continue to watch out for the temptation of becoming emotionally attached to someone other than your spouse. The first years of marriage are a time to adjust to each other. Sometimes those adjustments will come with conflict. While you should seek mentorship as you go through those adjustments, seek this help from individuals of the same sex or from a couple together. It is easy, for example, for a lady to find a listening ear in a male colleague at work. But sharing your marriage challenges creates an emotional attachment. It robs you as a couple of the emotional intimacy that should only be shared within your marriage. These emotional affairs also open the door for you to have a sexual affair. In our years working with couples, rarely have we come across a spouse who was unfaithful to their partner without it beginning as a seemingly innocent emotional attachment. That is why it is important to keep mutual couple friends and mentors to whom you can both be accountable.

Sex is most fulfilling when the two of you are spiritually connected. In the last chapter in this manual, we will discuss your dependence on

God's power for your marriage. You need God's power to experience the fulfilling sex life he intended. As you would pray persistently for anything in your marriage, do not forget to also pray persistently for your sex life! Take the time to ask God in prayer to prepare your bodies for each other. Pray about your fears and anticipation for sex in your marriage. Pray that you will both be sensitive to each other's sexual needs. Pray that you will experience fulfilment in your sex life.

As you prepare for sex in your marriage, prepare your body as well. Sex is not a passive activity; it takes physical strength. A healthy body will be more prepared for the strength needed in sex and to enjoy it. You can prepare your body now by making sure you are eating a balanced meal, getting the rest you need, and observing good hygiene. If you have not done this yet, we also encourage you to see your doctor for a physical check-up.

If you are considering using birth control, you will need to decide together what to use and prepare before the wedding day. A doctor can help you investigate different birth control methods. Take responsibility for your bodies and do your own research as well. Learn about the different birth control methods you are considering, how they work, and their side effects. There are methods that, instead of protecting you from conception, can prevent the fertilized egg from implanting in the uterus after conception. We also encourage you be a student of your body. Some birth control methods may have side effects, such as making the woman tired, reducing her appetite for sex, or causing mood swings. If you notice these affecting you, you may want to talk to a doctor about trying another method. There are birth control methods for men as well. As you go into marriage, be prepared to adjust to what will be comfortable and healthy for both of you. This is part of teamwork and a place to also affirm and take care of each other.

At the end of this chapter, we have recommended resources that will help you better prepare for sex in your upcoming marriage. You can also use them after you are married. These resources will address the physical, emotional, and spiritual aspects in sex. If you are carrying any burden as a result of your past sexual experiences or abuse, the resources will guide you in finding healing and reclaiming the joy of sex in marriage. Remember that you also have your mentors to walk with you. They are some of your most immediate resources, and they can also help you find more resources you might need.

Conclusion

No one goes into marriage having mastered secrets to sizzling sex. Each couple begins somewhere. Some couples begin on turbulence and others have smoother beginnings. Regardless of where you will begin, the goal is to continue to grow in your sexual intimacy. Like other aspects of your marriage, sexual intimacy is a beautiful and important experience that takes patience, teamwork, intentionality, and time. Going into it with willingness to learn and talk together is the beginning of a beautiful married sex life.

Digging Deeper

Individual Reflection

Find a quiet place with some privacy to complete this section. The aim of this activity is to help you identify areas you must choose to work on individually and let go of as you prepare for sexual intimacy in marriage.

1. As you prepare for your honeymoon night, what specific expectations are you anticipating for your sexual intimacy?
2. Can you think of any cultural attitudes toward sex that you have come to believe and could potentially help you or hinder you from experiencing a fulfilling sex life in your marriage?
3. Given the different messages our culture sends about what sex is for men and what it is for women, what potential problems do you foresee if you allow such rhetoric to influence you? How do you prepare to counter such rhetoric?
4. Have you considered if and what method of birth control you will use? If not, who do you need to ask for help with this decision?

Discussion

Meet together and complete this section. Make sure you choose a place where you can talk freely.

Go through your personal reflections together, taking turns to share how you answered the questions. Do not just give your answers. Let them guide you in having a healthy conversation on the subject of sex.

Prayer

Thank God for his goodness and for the good gift of sexual intimacy. Ask him to help you to serve and love each other with your bodies.

Mentors

Ask your mentor couple to tell you something they have learned about sexual intimacy. What advice do they have for you about your honeymoon?

Discuss birth control methods with your mentors. Which ones are you considering? Do they have advice that could guide you in your decision?

Take It Further

Make an appointment to visit a primary doctor for regular health check-up. At the appointment, ask the doctor for more information about the birth control you are considering.

Recommended Resources

- *Sheet Music: Uncovering the Secrets of Sexual Intimacy in Marriage* by Dr. Kevin Leman. The first four chapters give practical advice to couples preparing for marriage. They guard couples against making assumptions about what to expect in marriage. They help you understand differences – not only gender differences, but also differences in understanding what "good" sex means. We highly recommend you wait until after your wedding to read the rest of the chapters.

- *The Act of Marriage: The Beauty of Sexual Love* by Tim and Beverly LaHaye. You can start reading this book as you prepare for marriage. It has a wealth of information for you as you go through different stages in your marriage. This book provides some theological teachings about marriage and also practical advice on how to fulfil each other sexually in your marriage.
- *Intended for Pleasure: Sex Technique and Sexual Fulfillment in Christian Marriage* by Ed and Gaye Wheat. We recommend waiting until after your wedding to read this. The book discusses biblical teachings about sex and gives easy-to-understand medical advice about sex and sexuality. Its graphic illustrations teach you to better understand yourselves individually and also be proactive in how to please each other sexually.
- *Sexual Intimacy in Marriage* by William Cutrer and Sandra Glahn. This book is appropriate to begin as you prepare for your marriage. It discusses ways to achieve sexual pleasure in your marriage. It also discusses what biblically acceptable sexual activity in marriage looks like.
- *Overcoming Addictive Behavior* by Neil T. Anderson and Mike Quarles. If you are struggling with addictive sexual sin, you should start reading this book now. It helps you understand your addiction and guides you on how to overcome the addiction. It gives you suggested prayers and actions you could take to overcome the addiction.
- *Finding Freedom in a Sex-Obsessed World* by Neil T. Anderson. Whether you are struggling with sexual sin or want to better understand how to protect yourself against the pitfall, this book can help. The author discusses the guilt, anger, and fear that typically follow an individual who struggles with sexual sin. It guides you on how to free yourself from the emotional and

spiritual bondage resulting from sexual sin and gives practical steps to defeat sexual sin using the Word of God.

- *How Do I Escape the Trap of Pornography in My Life?* This article is written specifically to men, though it can also be applicable to women. It shares steps on how to protect yourself. If you are already caught in pornography, the steps will help you walk away and stand against its lure. **www.familylife.com/articles**
- *No Place to Cry* by Doris VanStone. This book offers hope to victims of sexual abuse, especially those who are struggling with emotional, physical, and spiritual pain as a result. Dorie shares how she suffered the pain of abuse from a tender age, how she chose forgiveness, and her journey to recovery.
- *On the Threshold of Hope: Opening the Door to Healing for Survivors of Sexual Abuse* by Diane Mandt Langberg. This book offers hope to both men and women who have survived the trauma of sexual abuse and guides the reader towards healing. Survivors write to remind abused people that they are not alone and that Christ is able to heal their deep wounds.
- *Recovering from Child Abuse: Healing and Hope for Victims* by David Powlison. This booklet is addressed to those who have suffered from abuse, including sexual abuse. The author highlights the emotional damage that comes with such abuse and how to work through those hurt emotions. This booklet is written by a counsellor who has worked with countless numbers of survivors of abuse and knows healing is possible.

9

Your New Family

Karembo's aunt said, "We have the suitcase ready, but it feels a bit too light." It had been empty when Jabali's family had dropped it off at Karembo's house a few days earlier. Tonight, they were picking up her "luggage" to symbolize that she was moving out of her home and her new family was excited to welcome her to their community.

The ladies from Jabali's family tried to make their way into the house. Karembo's family had posted a lady to guard the door who had a strong body to intimidate the women from Jabali's family. She shouted, "You cannot pass through this door until you make it clear why you are here. If you really want to take our girl to your home, show you are serious by paying a fee."

After a bit of teasing, someone paid to gain access, saying, "Nothing will stop us from getting our girl, not even if you demand a helicopter!" The ladies burst into the house, ululating.

One of Jabali's relatives carried the suitcase out, yelling, "She is moving to our homestead! Here is evidence that we are taking her with us!" Ladies from both families hugged and danced together until the suitcase was packed into a car waiting at the gate.

Then, both the guests and hosts sat under a tent outside to share a meal. The weather was perfect. The men had been busy roasting goat meat and chatting amongst themselves.

Jabali sat directly opposite one of Karembo's uncles. From the way people interacted with him, he was clearly influential in the family. *Karembo's family doesn't talk as much as mine*, Jabali thought. *Half the time I can't tell what they are thinking.* The uncle simply stared at him. *I feel like he can read my mind.* He averted his gaze. *Should I sit next to him? Or is it inappropriate to move before the ceremony is over? He will warm up to me once he sees I am a nice guy*, Jabali comforted himself as he turned to talk to his cousin.

From where Karembo sat, she could hear the ladies from Jabali's family. "That dress would look better on me," an aunt said.

"Do we have to wait for a wedding or a funeral to reunite us?" said a cousin. They interrupted each other and none of them seemed to take any offence.

Karembo could not imagine such conversations going on in her family. It would be deemed rude and intrusive. Her family cared for each other, but each minded their own business until asked. Karembo wondered, *How am I going to fit in to all this commotion? What if they think I am a silent snob? What if they hurt my feelings?*

Families in Transition

As you prepare to get married, it is not just the two of you who are getting ready to come together. Two families and two communities are preparing to come together. In one sense, you are both leaving your families of origin to build a new family. You are also being joined to another family that you did not grow up with. You will be navigating through two traditions and cultures to form your own.

As we have discussed before, you will each leave your father and mother and become one flesh with your new spouse (Genesis 2:24). Yet you still want to obey and honour your parents (Ephesians 6:1-3). As a couple, you will have opportunities to create and nurture relationships with your in-laws, bearing in mind that the goal in these relationships is to enhance your unity as a couple. This is also the time for you to nurture values, customs, and routines that you agree on as a couple and challenge those that could threaten your unity. It is a time for the two of you to start learning that you can honour your parents and still disagree with them.

Start preparing for this transition now, before you get married. This will help both of you begin to build a foundation that will define how you relate with your new family when you enter your marriage.

Leaving Your Family

Expect that it will take time and effort to gradually leave your own family. For example:

You will still be the same person that you were before you got married, carrying your background into this new family. The light switch does not automatically turn on and transform you into a different person. You will need to adjust to unfamiliar ways in your new family. When you interact with them and they respond differently from the way your own family responds, don't be surprised if you feel indifferent, upset, or confused by their response. It will take time and effort to remind yourself that you are in transition into a new family. You will also need to teach your new family about yourself because they are important to you. Reassure yourself that you will gradually learn how to adapt to them as they also learn how to adapt to you.

Your relationship with your parents will not change instantly. Both you and your parents will know in your heads that things have changed, but your hearts may still long for what you were used to. If your parents were always the go-to people in your life, you may be tempted to continue with this without involving your spouse. Depending on the season your parents may be in, you may be tempted to continue supporting them (financially or in other ways) the way you did before you got married. Remember, your parents have not moved on, it is you who has moved on. As you work together to agree how you should relate with your parents, you will slowly begin to redefine your relationship with your family.

If there were already conflicts in your birth family, they will not go away just because you got married. For example, if your family is poor at respecting your boundaries, they may continue with the same trend. If your family is distant and disconnected, they will not necessarily try to connect just because a new member has come into the family. You will need to work with the same good, bad, and ugly of your family as you enter your marriage.

Building Relationships with Your New In-laws

As you leave your family, you will also be gaining relationships with your spouse's family. Your relationship with your new family will not be the same as when you were dating. You will no longer be visiting as a guest. You will be part of the family and will be required to contribute to strengthen the family and actively participate in the social activities.

Because your marriage will involve more than the two of you, it is important for you, as a couple, to actively involve those two families and communities. Support from your future in-laws can make the transition more effective for both of you. You, therefore, need to agree to nurture those relationships. Paul told the Romans, "If it is possible, as far as it depends on you, live at peace with everyone" (Romans 12:18). This is the same message we charge you with as you begin to build relationships with your new family, both immediate and extended.

You will notice differences between you and them. Differences make sense because you did not grow up in the same home. They are welcoming you into their home with assumptions, and you may also be going into their family with assumptions. As you interact with your new family, you will begin to learn how true or false your assumptions are. They will teach you how things are done in their communities. You don't need to adopt all their ways, but these lessons can help to understand the family you are joining. You will also have the opportunity to teach them about you and your ways. Like any journey in life, your interaction will include encouraging and discouraging moments. Take it in stride and learn to grow with your new family, one experience at a time. To build a healthy relationship with anyone takes time and intentionality, but as you work on it, you will begin to see fruit.

Connecting with your new family is a way of appreciating what they did to raise your new spouse. Nurturing a relationship with your in-laws can also strengthen your relationship with your spouse. For instance, meeting together and sharing a meal with them can foster your unity as a couple and provide a place to build companionship with each other. As you socialize, you get to learn about your spouse's values, their way of doing things, and some answers to why they behave the way they do. A man who is intentional in building relationships with his in-laws will strengthen his relationship with his wife. When she notices him valuing what she cherishes, she will respond by building a stronger commitment to him. The same applies to a wife and her in-laws.

James does not wait for me (Chao) to reach out to my family. Time and again, he has been the one who encourages us to go visit my family. When they come to visit, he takes time off to serve them, drives them to where they need to go, and shares and researches ideas they need to hear. His love for my siblings definitely impacts the way I relate with him. In those challenging moments when my family has faced sickness, financial need, or family conflicts, it is easier to include him in those situations. I already know he cares for my family, which dissolves any possible tension about how we should be involved in the issues.

While some in-law relationships can be a burden to a couple, many are a blessing. Think of all the benefits a family offers. A family is there to celebrate and to protect you. A family gives you a sense of belonging and reminds you that we were made to live in community. Your in-laws are part of the community that will share time, knowledge, and material things with you. This is the family you will learn to call on when you have a sickness, a challenge, a dilemma, or even a disagreement that seems difficult to resolve between just the two of you. Why not start involving your in-laws in your marriage now?

Common Questions about In-laws

As you prepare to join a new family, you might ask:

What if this is not my first marriage or I have children?

For some of you, this is not your first marriage. You are coming in with influences from not only your family of origin, but also your previous relationship. Others may be coming into marriage as a single parent to a child or children. In some cases, the other birth parent may still want to be involved with the child. The biblical message about families does not change with your unique context, but you may have to think through how to apply it in your situation.

If you are bringing children into your marriage, you will be forming a blended family. A blended family is a family with unique dynamics. Both of you are coming into the marriage with assumptions that may be very different from each other. Appreciating those two worlds is one of the ways to help build your own marriage and be part of this new family. You will need to learn how to include the children in the building of this new family. If you isolate them, you may end up making it more difficult to build unity in your marriage. After all, the children are yours and you cannot give them up as someone else's responsibility.

Remember, too, that your intended is not only preparing to build relationships with your spouse's parents and siblings, he or she is also getting ready to build relationships with your children. Discuss together how you can allow your unique situation to build, not destroy, your unity as a couple.

What if my in-laws try to "run my life"?

Everything is a process. Severing the umbilical cord is not easy. It can be harder with certain dynamics in the family. A single mother may be more reluctant to let go of her child partly because of the unique challenges involved in single parenting. If the father in the home took the back seat and the mother had to provide for the family, the mother's involvement with her now-married child could feel like she is asserting her position, even in her child's new home. Some parents call family meetings and expect their children to show up without giving them ample time to plan. You may be the only one who has been there for your parents. If you have other siblings, it is time to get them on board so that you can share the responsibility. Help your family understand that you are about to start your marriage and things will need to change. Include your intended in the conversations. In all this, be sure to honour your parents even when you disagree with them.

What if one of us doesn't easily warm up to our new in-laws?

It's possible you may feel overwhelmed, uncomfortable, and even conflicted at gatherings with your new in-laws. It is not unusual for tension to exist with in-laws when you are newly married. But you cannot avoid visits and interaction with your new family.

It helps to talk about it. Wishing it away will not solve the issue. Confront the issue together. It is important to build relationships with your new in-laws. If you can actively engage in this, it will help. This is also an area you can discuss with your mentors. Remember you and your intended other are both trying to learn about each other.

Consider working out a compromise on family gatherings together. What can you do together to ease some of the stress and tension you experience during those gatherings? For instance, you could be involved in the gatherings but make sure there are breaks. Perhaps you can spend the day with the family, and in the evening spend the night somewhere else. This will help the one who is uncomfortable to recuperate and reenergize for the next day.

What if our families have different traditions?

Don't assume that you know everything about the culture you are marrying into. You will find some traditions are so ingrained that people do not even notice they are doing them. For example, your in-laws may have a taboo that a married man cannot sleep in his parents' home. To avoid this, the family will make quick arrangements to have their son put up a house, even if it is temporary, before he travels to the village.

You may find traditions that are unfamiliar to you or that you disagree with. Some traditions may not run contrary to your beliefs but rather to your preferences. It is helpful to distinguish between agreeing with something and preferring not to be involved in it.

Start the conversation now about your traditions and how you will do things. If you are coming into the marriage with fewer traditions, you might feel that your spouse is not working with you as a team or that they care about their family more than about you. This is not a competition. Give your spouse the benefit of the doubt. Leave the door open to ask questions and agree on how to handle such situations as they come.

What if my future in-laws are not Christians?

Not everyone marries into a Christian home. You may be marrying into a home that leans towards more traditional cultural beliefs or a different religion. The difference in beliefs may be more pronounced during family gatherings. It is a delicate challenge to be a witness for your faith while still maintaining respect and valuing the relationship. On the one hand, you need to show God's love to your non-Christian in-laws. On the other, you need to help them realize that you will build your marriage on different values.

It can be easier for the one who is from the family of non-Christians to encourage dialogue and share why you cannot join them in some family activities that contradict your beliefs. Additionally, remember to:

Pray for them. Prayer changes circumstances and people. Pray for your non-Christian in-laws. Pray for their salvation. Pray for opportunities to build relationships with them and show them Christ.

Check your attitude. Be sure your attitude is one of love and humility, not of pride and arrogance. Much as you may try, you cannot change them. Even when you invite them to Christian activities, let your goal not be to convert them. Only the Holy Spirit can convert someone.

Simply share your faith. In words and in deeds, share your faith with them. Let them see and hear Christ in the way you relate with each other and others in the community.

Creating a New Family

Your transition from your family of origin into the family you and your spouse will create not only gives you the opportunity to build relationships with your in-laws, it also gives you the opportunity to create a new culture for your own home. This new culture will be instrumental in defining your values. It will help you build unity, both as a couple and also with the children you will bring into the family. It will also enhance your sense of belonging in a family unit.

One of the ways to create your new family is by beginning to build traditions together. You can choose traditions or routines that you observe on a daily basis, such as holding devotions every morning or evening. Weekly traditions might include agreeing that Fridays are game nights or movie nights for the family. You can also create holiday traditions, where you agree what you will do, where you will go, and with whom. Perhaps it is April holidays at the village where not only the two of you but also your extended family is involved. It might be a mid-year holiday where you choose to get away just you as a family, far from the rest of the extended family. Or perhaps you choose to celebrate Christmas at your house and make short visits to family members nearby. Whatever way you do it, it helps create a sense of order. Your tradition becomes something to look forward to – not only for the two of you, but also for your children when you have them.

The two of you, as husband and wife, can discuss and agree about how to make decisions in your home. These decisions may or may not be in agreement with your families of origin. For example, this is a good time to decide the number of children you would like to have, the names you will give them, and your parenting styles. You have the time to talk about parenting aspects you learned from your families of origin that you would like to keep, those you would like to let go of, and those you would like to add on to.

We have tried to build some value in our home that neither of us grew up with. For instance, we chose to be present to support one another in our different areas of passion, skills, and giftings. Both our children have played football since they were five years old. They are passionate and skilled players. From the beginning, Chao and I (James) agreed that unless a game conflicted with a mandatory assignment, we would make sure we watched them play. Additionally, every morning before the children left for school, we would spend about 15 minutes reading a short devotional, after which each one of us would say a short prayer. We did not need to remind each other – it was our routine.

Every married couple creates a new family when they start their new home. Some are intentional about it, others are not. Being intentional about creating your new family gives you the opportunity to work together as a team that builds your unity as a married couple.

As you prepare to create your new family, here are some guidelines you may find useful:

- Who is this tradition or routine for? Is it for just the two of you as a couple, the children, or your whole family? Are your in-laws involved?
- When and where will you create and build this culture? Will it be in your home, away from home, with your extended family, or with other friends? Will you observe it on a daily, weekly, or periodical basis?
- How do you begin? Starting with a tradition that includes just the two of you is more practical than one that involves the children you have not had yet, or your in-laws.

Jabali and Karembo Dive In

"Karembo, did you not hear that?" one of her girlfriends whispered. "They are waiting for you to walk to the front and sit with Jabali on those two chairs." Karembo had been buried in her thoughts again.

An uncle said, "These two young people are the reason we are here. We joyfully give you our daughter and also joyfully receive your son as ours. You can see how well we took care of her. Her face is smooth, she is healthy, and you can see how happy she looks. We trust that, if anything will change under your care, it will be that she will glow even more."

As the speeches, hugs, and handshakes continued, Karembo's mood lifted. Despite their differences, the two families were united in the joy of celebrating their wedding.

At 9 p.m., the master of ceremonies announced: "A celebration is not a celebration until people have eaten. Please do not be in a hurry to leave. There is plenty of food to go around, and it was prepared with you in mind."

Before Jabali made his way to the table reserved for the wedding party, he visited with some of Karembo's family. "Young man," Karembo's uncle called out to Jabali, "tell me again what you do for a living." He motioned Jabali to sit on the empty chair next to him. "You have chosen well, young man. Looks like she chose well too."

Karembo was glad when she spotted the two of them engaged in deep conversation. She had always liked her uncle's reflective personality. *True, he's a bit strange*, she thought, *but he's the best uncle I could ask for!*

Inspired by Jabali, Karembo told herself, *I can make the best of being in this family, or I can start with my own suspicions.* She walked over to some ladies from Jabali's family who had come from out of town.

The more they interacted, the more comfortable they became. By the end of the night, Karembo was hugging and thanking them all for coming to celebrate. Jabali waved the uncle farewell as he directed traffic. *What a wonderful night after all.*

Conclusion

As you prepare to leave your family of origin, start your own family, and begin to build relationships with your in-laws, you will be preparing to do what many, including your parents, have done and will continue to do. Like any human relationship that needs to grow, it is a process that takes time and some adjusting. It is also a lifetime process because it does not necessarily end.

Relationships and community give us a sense of belonging, either in our own homes or in our extended families. Knowing this will help you not only look forward to, but also be intentional in building those relationships. As Africans, we believe that relationships are our wealth, that meaning is found in relationships and not in material things. Investing in those relationships is, therefore, an addition and not a depletion to your wealth.

The process of adjusting into your new family is both rewarding and challenging. While you might be willing to approach your new family with great joy and expectation, some of your in-laws may not be nearly as excited. They might be unsure about the changes that will come with you joining their family, especially how it will affect their relationship with your spouse. To mitigate some of these challenges, remember that you are not going in to make a replica of your family of birth. Embracing the differences you will find in your new family and slowly finding your place among them will be more rewarding.

Unity between the two of you as a couple will help you further work through any discomfort or conflict that might occur between you and your new family. Taking care of each other, creating your own family values, and being united in your decisions will also help you to be more intentional in engaging with your in-laws. This is, therefore, a time for you to not only prepare yourselves as individuals, but also to prepare yourselves as a couple. It is a time for you to look forward to the joy of belonging to a new family.

Digging Deeper

Individual Reflection

Find a place with some privacy to complete this section. The aim of this activity is to help you better prepare to build relationships with your new family.

1. Refer to the love letter you wrote after chapter 5, Communicating through Conflict. What were some of the traits that attracted you to the one you are about to marry? Is it possible that their family nurtured the environment for them to grow in those traits?
2. As a way to thank their family, write them a letter thanking them for raising the person you are about to marry. You will not need to show them this letter if it is not appropriate or feasible. Remember to be specific about the areas you are thanking them for. Some examples include their generosity, cooking skills, servant attitude, how they are easy to talk to, etc.

Discussion

Meet together and complete this section. Make sure you choose a place where you can talk freely.

Take turns reading the letter you wrote to each other's families. Discuss the letters and share what stood out for you.

As you prepare to be joined to your spouse and to also start to build relationships with their family, what are you looking forward to? What are some of the fears or concerns about this transition into your new family?

Prayer

Pray for your parents, your in-laws, and your relatives as you prepare to get married. Pray for all that this transition will mean for them. Pray for your relationships with them and that you will love them well.

Mentors

Ask your mentors what surprised them about the other person's family.

What adjustments have they had to make? What have they appreciated about their in-laws?

Take It Further

Visit an older relative (from both sides) who you find easy to talk to.

During your visit, ask questions to help you learn more about your family heritage and traditions.

10

Depending on God

It was time for Jabali and Karembo to exchange their vows. Jabali looked radiant. The African fabric gave his half coat flair and added accents to his trousers and shoes. Karembo's white dress had a beaded waistline and matching head crown. Instead of jewellery for her neck, she had hints of beaded calabashes that matched the beads on the waistline. She looked like royalty.

As they prepared to exchange their vows, the officiating pastor said to Jabali and Karembo, "What you are about to share with each other, in this room full of witnesses, will define and shape the marriage you are about to begin." They locked their fingers together.

Karembo's sister, her maid of honour, had joked, "I will be so mad at you if you cry and mess up your make-up!" Karembo thought she could hold it together, but she wasn't sure about Jabali. He cleared his throat, but his words were still stuck there. Karembo squeezed his hand and nodded. By the end of the vows, several of the bridesmaids and groomsmen were grateful for the box of tissues on the table where Jabali and Karembo would soon sign their marriage certificate.

Towards the end of the ceremony, the pastor said, "We now invite the couple's parents and mentors to come forward and surround the couple." The best man placed two pillow cushions on the staircase leading to the altar for Jabali and Karembo to kneel on as they were prayed for.

Karembo's father finished his prayer using words from Isaiah 26:3: "Lord, I pray Jabali and Karembo will choose to depend on you, that they will choose to trust in you, and that as they do this, they will find your perfect peace for their marriage." Karembo's mind flooded with all the things she had worried about throughout their engagement. How she had longed for peace! But God offered her this promise if she and Jabali just depended on God in their marriage. Karembo gave up on preserving her make-up and finally let the tears flow.

This chapter discusses dependence on God in marriage and challenges you to evaluate your individual relationships with Jesus Christ. If you do not have that relationship yet, it guides you in making a commitment to begin this relationship. If you already have a relationship with Jesus Christ, this chapter encourages you to continue to grow in your intimacy with Christ and with each other by depending on the power of the Holy Spirit.

Why God Needs to Be the Centre of Your Marriage

A careful look at the Bible shows that God, in the beginning, instituted a marriage between Adam and Eve. God himself fashioned Eve and brought her to Adam (Genesis 2:22), and the two became the first couple. In the book of Revelation, the last book in the Bible, God uses marriage to symbolize the union between Christ and the church (Revelation 19:9; 21:9; 22:17), a union Christ uses to show couples how they ought to love one another (Ephesians 5:25). God is the one who instituted marriage, and he is the one who regulates it. Knowing the one who instituted marriage and walking according to its regulation will give you, as a couple, all the benefits for your union.

This is why your success in marriage is directly dependent on your relationship with Jesus Christ. The late literary writer Chinua Achebe talked about how when the centre is weak, things fall apart. For people to stand strong, they need to affirm and unite around values. We add to what he says by stating that Jesus is the centre of everything. He is the one who holds everything together. He is the foundation on whom we build our lives, our marriages. If that centre, that foundation, is lacking, then *things fall apart*. This does not have to be the case. There is another way, and it begins with a relationship with Jesus Christ.

In working with couples, we have interacted with those who said they do not need Christ because they are happily married without him. When we ask them how they have managed to have a happy marriage, they share how they work hard to practice principles including forgiveness, patience, unity. Unknowingly, they practice principles that are rooted in Christ, though they practice the principles out of self-will. Without Jesus as Lord of your life, your marriage becomes an effort that the two of you will strive to make in your own strength.

Some of these couples have later subscribed to a biblical marriage. They will tell you it was transformational to intentionally depend on God to give them the strength and the faith to practice those principles. Instead of striving and depending on themselves, couples who depend on God in their marriage will find that he gives them everything they need to build their marriage. There are times when your strength will fail you, but God's strength is always available; it never runs out.

What does this look like in marriage? There will be times when you will be tempted to depend on each other for satisfaction in life. Much as you might try, you will find out that you are incapable of completely satisfying each other. The only one who can give you everything you need is Christ, by the power of his Holy Spirit. The two of you can continue to build interdependence where you have a mutual reliance on each other. However, if you begin to depend on the other person to meet all your needs and longings, you put your intended other in the place of God. Only God is fully dependable. He is the only strong anchor that is not dependent on anything to stand. Putting your intended other in a position to meet all your needs and longings is a set-up for failure – for both of you. As you have already seen in other chapters, you are both coming in with needs and limitations, and that is why you need to learn how to complete each other and work through those areas.

God's love also enables you to love your spouse. In moments when you are tempted not to love your intended other, the Holy Spirit will be there to remind you that according to 1 John 4:19, "We love because he first loved us." The knowledge that you are already loved and forgiven by Christ affirms you as a person and gives you the strength to pour yourself out to your intended other. You, therefore, give yourself fully to each other, knowing that the source for your love, Jesus, can never be increased or decreased; it is always a perfect love. In moments when your intended other does not show that kind of love, you are quick to remind yourself that, whether you see it or not, you are perfectly loved by Christ.

When you need to forgive in marriage, the Holy Spirit gives you the power to forgive. In moments when you wrong your intended other and they are having difficulty forgiving you, even as you wait for her or his heart to grow tender, you already know that you are already forgiven in Christ. In moments when you are having a hard time forgiving yourself, you can draw the conclusion that, if Christ has already forgiven you, then you also can choose to forgive yourself.

Whether you are coming into this marriage having witnessed struggling marriages in your parents or those around you, you can still have a strong marriage. You can choose to build your marriage with the help of the Creator of marriage himself. Understanding what marriage is according to the Bible will strengthen your marriage and deepen your understanding of the gospel. The Holy Spirit will be there to affirm you as you celebrate life together and to strengthen and teach you in those challenging moments. The Holy Spirit will give you peace and guidance in your marriage. As you depend on God, you will find power to navigate the challenges of day-to-day married life and implement the practical solutions to marriage difficulties. We pray that you will make it a daily choice to depend on the Holy Spirit for the growth of your marriage.

My Story

I, Chao, grew up in a religious home. Our parents made sure we attended church and participated in different church activities. During my last two years of high school, as I faced the joys and challenges of growing up and prepared for the college entry exams, I became aware of an emptiness that nothing could fill. I tried to fill the emptiness by performing well in school, being good to others, and getting more involved in different church activities. Whenever I was in a crisis, I cried out to God for help. As soon as I felt relieved, I went back to my life of performance. One day, as I went through another bout of emptiness, a friend told me about a relationship with Jesus. On that day, she led me through a prayer to invite Jesus to be Lord and Saviour over my life. That was the beginning of my journey to allow Jesus to take control of my life.

My individual decision to depend on Jesus is foundational in the attitude I have in my marriage. With Christ in control, my purpose in marriage is firmly grounded. I am aware that Christ is the answer to those moments of emptiness. Christ, not my marriage, defines me. He gives me worth, strength, and joy in my marriage. I know I can depend on God to teach me, for example, how to respect my husband, even when I disagree with him. Christ helps me to choose to see James as Christ sees him. My dependence on God helps me submit to James (Ephesians 5:22); it helps James love me as Christ loved the church and gave himself for it (5:25).

Depending on God has also helped James and me through the challenges we have faced in marriage. Marriage was a lot harder than we expected. I vividly remember at our wedding ceremony when we asked the rest of the congregation to join us in singing the hymn, "Great Is Thy Faithfulness". We did not know then, and we could not have predicted, how applicable the song would become as we faced challenges in building our marriage. In one of the stanzas, the hymnist says:

> Pardon for sin and a peace that endureth,
> Thine own dear presence to cheer and to guide,
> Strength for today and bright hope for tomorrow –
> Blessings all mine, with ten thousand beside!

It is through God that we have walked in a peace that endures the challenges in marriage. When we have needed cheering and guiding in our marriage, we have only found it in our dependence on God. When we have felt weak and hopeless in our marriage, our dependence on God has continued to remind us that we are a blessed couple, as we look to God.

Our Story of Learning to Depend on God

Making the decision to call Jesus Lord over your life is the beginning of the adventure of marriage as God intended for it to be. After deciding to come to Jesus and call him Lord and Saviour over your life, the Holy Spirit comes to live inside you. John 14:26 reminds us that the Holy Spirit is sent by God to be our helper and our teacher, who reminds us of everything Jesus has said. This means that as you grow in your marriage, you always have access to help! As you choose to walk by the power of the Holy Spirit, he will help both of you to love one another as Christ calls you to, to forgive each other when you need to, and to build each other in your marriage.

In the first six months of our marriage, I (Chao) noticed something that I thought needed to change, but I was not sure how to bring it up with James. On most weekends, James and his friends would watch a game of football or basketball at one of their homes. While I was happy that he kept this habit with his friends, we hardly had time just the two of us. On weekdays, we would leave home early for work and come back late in the evening. On some Saturdays, James would spend most of the afternoon helping out at church. That left us with Sunday afternoons to have time just the two of us – but that was when most of the games were on. Before we knew it, another week would start, and the cycle would repeat itself.

I was beginning to feel resentful towards James. I asked the Holy Spirit to help me know how to bring up the issue with wisdom and respect, so James would see I was not opposed to him watching sports or spending time with his friends. I wanted James to see that it was because I loved him and wanted us to have time with each other. I noticed my attitude towards the conversation change.

When Chao confronted me (James), I was ready to defend myself. I felt like replying that when I was at church, I was doing the work of God, that Chao did not like my friends, or that Chao should be thankful that I spent my free time in the "right places" and was not out getting in trouble like "other husbands" we knew.

However, as I listened to her, I first breathed spiritually. Breathing spiritually means that I allow the Holy Spirit to strengthen me and direct me in how I should respond. I asked Chao to forgive me for not prioritizing our marriage during my free time. I realized my relationship with my friends, while I hoped it would continue to grow, would need to change because I had one more person I needed to be in agreement with as I made decisions. As Chao and I worked towards resolving this conflict, I admitted to her that we needed to work as a team. I also admitted I needed the Holy Spirit to guide me in my new commitment. Given how defensive I felt at first, I know that my response to Chao of affirming her, affirming our relationship, and committing to change came from the power of the Holy Spirit.

In every situation where Chao and I have chosen to respond to the power of the Holy Spirit in our marriage, he has proven dependable.

Cultivate Your Dependence on the Holy Spirit's Power

Two people who trust Jesus for salvation have access to the Holy Spirit's power. Walking by the power of the Holy Spirit is a daily decision you make as individuals and also as a couple. If you are like us and many couples we have worked with, you have not fully allowed the Holy Spirit to take control over your lives and relationship. One of the ways to cultivate this dependence on the Holy Spirit's power is by studying the Word of God and praying together.

The Bible, if unopened, is no more powerful in your life than any other book you have on your shelf. But if you choose to open it regularly, read it, and apply to your life what you are reading, then you reap the benefits. Opening the Bible, reading it, and applying it to your marriage will not come easily. Being intentional and making it a priority will take willingness and discipline. In Psalm 119:103, the psalmist declares his love for the Word of God by saying, "How sweet are your words to my taste, sweeter than honey to my mouth!" As you go into marriage, you will experience many sweet moments. While you should treasure those sweet moments, choosing to taste the sweetness of the Word of God and savouring it in your marriage is a habit that will make those other moments in your marriage even sweeter.

The goal is to start together and make adjustments as you go. Do not be intimidated by the magnitude of the commitment. See it as a time for the two of you to be in the company of Christ, inviting him to teach you how to depend on him in your marriage. You can choose to read and discuss a book in the Bible together. You can commit to reading a few verses and discussing them. As God leads you, you can pray using those specific verses. If you are not ready to read the Bible together verse by verse, you can do what Wole and Destiny ended up doing.

Wole and Destiny

Before they got married, Wole and Destiny were disciplined in reading the Bible and in individual Bible study. "I used to wake up early, read my Bible, and pray before I did anything else," Destiny shared. A few months into their marriage, Wole says, "Mornings became busy as we hurried to go to work. We took a minute or two to pray for each other and off we went." When they came home in the evening after having been in traffic for at least an hour, they felt they did not have the energy to concentrate on reading the Bible.

One day at a bookstore, Destiny bought a book called *Daily Devotionals for Couples*. Each devotional had a verse of Scripture, a paragraph to reflect on it, and a suggestion on how they could together pray using the Scripture. She was not sure what Wole would think. Wole says, "We agreed to try it. Soon enough, we were in the habit of reading a devotional a night." It could take as little as 15 minutes, but they could discuss further if they had more time. Destiny added, "Reading those brief chapters and holding a brief discussion was easier to do."

Wole and Destiny slowly moved on to reading a book of the Bible together. "Sometimes we don't get to it because we are caught up in so many other things. But then we miss those moments together and look for time to continue with the discipline," Destiny said. They now have two children. Wole says, "Some seasons are easier than others, but we make an effort to protect that special time together." Even when they pray and read the Bible with their children, the time together just the two of them as a couple is still a priority.

Like anything else in marriage, it takes work and discipline to grow together in Christ. Dependence on God is a habit that can be cultivated when the two of you are committed to making the time and effort. Wole and Destiny found a useful tool that worked for them. In the section titled **Further Resources** on page 197, you will find more suggested tools that you can use to grow together in your dependence on Christ.

Surround Yourselves with Like-minded People

This does not mean you walk away from relationships with your single friends. Single or married, we are all part of the family of God and we need each other. Granted, your single friends may not identify with your stage of life in marriage, but you both still need each other's fellowship and prayers for each other. Also surrounding yourselves with like-minded couples gives you people who can identify with what you are going through. No marriage is perfect. Learning from each other as each couple grows in their marriage is an added advantage. You are also able to meet others who will mentor you and other couples you will have the privilege of mentoring.

Precious and Solomon

We mentored Precious and Solomon as they prepared for marriage and encouraged them to visit when they got back from their honeymoon and had settled into a routine.

As we visited over a meal, they shared about the adjustments they were making in their first six months of marriage. "We are finding it hard to make our relationships with our other couple friends meaningful," Precious admitted. Once a month, they would invite other couples over. Solomon said, "When we meet, we talk about our careers, and we challenge each other with different ways to invest financially. I like this a lot. But I feel what is missing is how we challenge each other to grow in our walk with God for our marriages."

We shared some discipleship tools for couples with Precious and Solomon, which you can find in the list of **Further Resources** on page 197. They settled on a basic tool that did not require much preparation time and would help them discuss one area of marriage at a time. Years into their marriage, Solomon and Precious have continued to build accountability with like-minded couples using the same tool. They have also mentored other couples to do the same, and the couples they have mentored have also mentored several other couples.

Marriage was not meant to be lived out in isolation. Therefore, do not isolate yourselves from others. Come together with like-minded couples to access tools that will help you grow in your dependence in God. It is very likely that as you grow together with other couples, God will bring to you others who need this same kind of help. You will be in a position to share your stories and tools with them.

Conclusion

I (Chao) have shared with you about my decision to ask Jesus to be Lord and Saviour over my life. It has made a huge difference in my personal life and also in my married life. Our prayer for you is that you would know the Father who designed marriage; Jesus, who provided the ultimate picture of love when he sacrificed his life for ours; and the Holy Spirit, whose power enables us to sustain our relationships. We pray that you would experience the full blessing that comes from making God the strong centre who holds together your lives and your marriage.

We recognize that some of you may still be contemplating whether you would like Jesus to become the centre and foundation of your life. This decision is the basis of everything else we have shared in this book. Yet it is very simple. In Romans 10:9, Paul said to his readers: "If you declare with your mouth, 'Jesus is Lord,' and believe in your heart that God raised him from the dead, you will be saved." Simply by saying and believing this, you are assured of eternal life! Would you prayerfully consider this decision? If you still have questions, talk to your mentors about them.

Digging Deeper

Individual Reflection

Find a quiet place with some privacy to complete this section. The aim of this activity is to help you work through your commitment to follow Jesus and to help you build your dependence on God, by the power of his Holy Spirit.

As you reflect on your life, has there been a time when you prayed to Jesus and asked him to be Lord and Saviour over your life? If yes, briefly write down how this happened and be prepared to share with your intended other when you meet for discussion. If not, is this something you would like to do?

Discussion

Meet together and complete this section. Make sure you choose a place where you can talk freely.

Go through your individual reflections together, taking turns to share how you answered the questions. Do not just state your answers, let them guide you in having a healthy conversation about dependence in God.

As you go into marriage, discuss some of what you would like to do together to grow in your dependence on God. See if you can come up with at least two ways.

Prayer

If you have asked Jesus to be your Lord and Saviour, take a moment now to thank Jesus for his salvation. You can do this by saying this simple prayer:

> *Dear God, I thank you for the salvation that I have in your Son, Jesus Christ. Jesus, I thank you for going to the cross, shedding your blood, and dying for my sins. I thank you that I have an intimate relationship with you. I thank you that I can depend on you for every area of my life. I look to you to continue to build my faith and trust in you. Amen.*

If you would like to begin a relationship with Jesus, you can pray a simple prayer like this:

> *Dear God, I admit I am a sinner and need your forgiveness. I believe that Jesus Christ went to the cross, shed his blood, and died for my sins. I choose to turn away from my sins. I invite you to come into my heart and life and be my Lord and Saviour. Amen.*

Mentors

Ask your mentor couple how they have depended on God in their marriage.

What difference has this made? What practices would they recommend to you for depending on God in marriage?

Take It Further

Find a gift for your mentor couple. As you present the gift, share how meeting with them has impacted you.

11

And the Story Goes On . . .

The wedding church service was over. The newlyweds walked down the aisle hand in hand. The ululating was deafening: *lililili lilililili lili*. The crowd was uncontrollable with excitement. The ladies had already gathered outside the reception hall to receive the newlyweds as they made their way to the high table.

Karembo shouted in Jabali's direction, "I can't believe it is done."

The master of ceremony tried to get people's attention by promising them, "We will have more time to dance. Right now, we need to get the newlyweds seated so that we can pray for the food." The crowd would have none of that. As the newlyweds made their way to their seats, one of Karembo's aunties pulled them into the dancing train that had already formed. Up they went, down they danced, jumping high and clapping.

One of Jabali's friends called out, "It is not always that we get to celebrate a wedding, so let's do it well!" By the time the master of ceremony managed to quiet down the crowd and get everyone seated, it was obvious that the dust had been shaken.

As Jabali helped Karembo to her seat, he could not help but think: *Today marks the end of me and the beginning of us*. Karembo was also in her own world: *Here comes a new chapter in my life*.

They soaked it all in, celebrating each other with the family and friends who had stood with them through their months of preparation for this special day. Before they knew it, they were off to their honeymoon. The wedding was over, but their story had just begun.

Jabali and Karembo went on to move into their new home. It took longer than they had planned, but eventually they moved in. They had built a foundation for their home, with expansion in mind. Initially, they only focused on what they could afford to build. Before they moved in, they built two rooms and a bathroom. While in their home, they continued to expand into other rooms, as the money become available. By the time they started having children, they had the other rooms done and an additional bathroom. Karembo told her mother when she stopped by to visit, "We can have couple friends over on weekends, and they can come with their children!"

For the past several sessions with this manual, you have been building your marriage before it begins. You have done what you can with the time that you have. We are excited for you to enjoy your new home together! Find reasons to laugh, reasons to celebrate each other, and reasons to love more deeply each day. In the end, no relationship outside of an intimacy with God is deeper and more meaningful than the marriage relationship.

From blissful memories to the challenges we've faced, James and I (Chao) have found that marriage lived out on a godly foundation is beautiful. We're confident you will find the journey wonderful because you already have laid a strong foundation. You will continue to build upon it, one brick at a time. Like Jabali and Karembo who had enough room to share with those who would stop by, your marriage will benefit not only you, but also those in your circle. What a joyful reward!

Chao and I (James) have shared with you what we have learned as we have grown in our marriage. It's our passion to see couples thrive in their marriages, to the extent that they can help other couples thrive in their marriage. We invite you to join us in this passion. As you go into your marriage, you have a foundation laid. You have enough of what you need to help another couple thrive. Start by being intentional in sharing with others about the lessons you carried with you during your season of preparing for your marriage. Tell them how you are utilizing what you learned. We're excited to see how God will use your testimony to help others thrive in their preparations and marriages.

Our Prayer for You:

Dear heavenly Father,

We pray for each man and woman who has made a commitment to prepare for their marriage. As they begin their marriage, we pray that they will choose you as their first priority for their lives. We pray that they will choose to pursue intimacy with you before anything else. We pray that they will choose to make their marriage their second priority after you, that they will water their garden of marriage, that they will choose to enjoy and not endure their marriage, that they will choose to work on their marriage by choosing to give it the time and commitment it needs. We pray that in their fun moments, they will experience overwhelming fun. In difficult moments, we pray they will choose to hold on to you together. We pray that their marriage will be the open Bible many couples will read and as they read, that they will be drawn to you, because they see these couples live out your purpose for marriages.

In Jesus's name we pray!

Chao and James

Activities and Resources

Personal History Data

The first exercise helps you understand your background, how it affects your relationship with your intended other, and how it can affect how you build your marriage. During the sessions, most of the information you filled out will come up. You will determine what to carry with you into your marriage and what to leave behind. You will also be challenged to work through any conflict you might still have regarding your past.

If you are going through this manual with a mentor couple, fill this out before your first meeting if possible and bring it with you. You will have the opportunity to discuss your answers.

If you are working through the manual just the two of you, this Personal History Data will guide you in better understanding both yourself and each other. When you each are done filling it out, sit together and share your answers with each other.

Personal History Data

Name: ______________________ Age: ______________________

Occupation: ____

How long have you worked with your current employer? ____________

Your highest level of education completed: ____________________

Were you previously married? _____ If yes, how many times? _________

Are you divorced or widowed? _____ For how long? _______________

Do you have children? ___________ If yes, how many? _____________

Your current church affiliation: ______________________

Past church affiliation: ______________________

Your Current Relationship History

1. How did you meet? ______________________

2. What attracted you to him or her? ______________________

3. How long have you been dating? ______________________

4. Do you have a wedding date planned? If yes, when and where will your wedding take place? ______________________

5. Do you have children in this current relationship? ______________________

6. How do your parents and siblings feel about your relationship?

7. Do they know of your plans to get married? ____________

   How are you planning to involve them in your wedding plans and day? ____________

8. If one or both of your parents are not present, who are you planning to take their positions as you plan your visits and on the day of your wedding? How did you come to that decision? ____________

Your Past Relationships

1. Have you had a serious dating relationship in the past? If so, how did you meet? ____________

2. What good and bad memories do you have of your past relationship? ____________

3. How and why did the relationship end? ____________

4. Do you have children from any of your past relationships? If yes, how many? ___

___

___

If You Have Been Married Before

1. Did you have children in your previous marriage? ___

   If yes, how many and how old are they? ___

2. If you are divorced, what were your reasons for the divorce?

   ___

   ___

   ___

3. Did you try to work out your differences before you divorced?

   ___

   If so, how? ___

   ___

   ___

   Do you still talk to each other? ___ Please explain your answer. ___

   ___

   What have you done to heal from your past marriage? ___

   ___

   ___

   ___

4. Is there anything you still need to work through to heal from this past relationship? ________ Please explain your answer. ________

____

____

5. If you are widowed, how did your spouse pass away? ________

____

____

Were there any significant conflicts you had with your spouse that you feel you have not dealt with? If yes, please explain. ________

____

____

What have you done to help you heal from your loss? ________

____

____

Family History

1. In addition to your siblings, were you raised with other relatives? If yes, please explain your relationship and how many they were.

____

____

____

2. What are your favourite memories of growing up? ________

____

____

____

What was the most difficult period in your growing up? Please explain your answer. ______

______

______

3. If you grew up with both your parents, who was the obvious head of the home and how did they show their authority or leadership?

______

______

______

How is your relationship with your parents and siblings? Please explain your answer. ______

______

______

______

Are there any unresolved issues between you and both or one of your parents or siblings? Please explain your answer. ______

______

______

______

Spiritual Inventory

1. What kind of spiritual upbringing did you grow up in? ______

______

______

______

2. Currently, what role does God play in your life? ______

______

______

______

3. When you die, where do you think you will go and why? ______

______

______

______

What effect has your relationship with each other had on your spiritual life? Please explain. ______

______

______

______

4. Are you involved in anything that helps you grow spiritually?

______

______

______

5. If you attend church, how are you involved in the church community? ______

______

______

______

Couples Interview

One of the ways we learn about marriage is by listening to couples who are already married. One of the ways to listen authentically is by asking specific questions. This exercise is meant to do exactly that. Find two couples you look up to who have been married for at least five years. One of the couples could be your mentor couple. Other couples could be those you know from your church or other social groups. Find a comfortable place where you can visit over tea or a light meal. Some couples would prefer you visit them at home. Go prepared to take notes, ask questions, and enjoy the visit. When you are done with the interview, make time where the two of you can sit and discuss some of your take-aways from the interview with the couples.

1. When and how did you meet?
2. What attracted you to each other?
3. How long did you date before you proposed? How did you propose?
4. When you agreed to get married, who are some of the first people you told? How did you arrive at the decision to tell them first?
5. When you took her or him to visit your family, what was your family's response? Was this an official visit to introduce yourselves to the family or did you make frequent visits? Please explain your answer.
6. During the marriage negotiation period, how did you get the rest of your family to stand with you? Was the support primarily emotional or was it also financial? What lessons did you learn

during that season? If you were to do it again, would you do it any differently? If yes, how? And if no, how come?

7. What drove your wedding budget and how did you fund your wedding?
8. What are some of the memories you treasure for your first year of marriage?
9. What are some of the greatest areas of conflict during your first year of marriage? How did you learn to resolve them?
10. What role does God play in your marriage? How do you specifically see him build your marriage?
11. As we prepare for our marriage, what three things would you encourage us to be aware of during our first few years of marriage?

Parents Interview

This questionnaire is for you to give to your parents or the guardians who raised you. Filling out answers in writing can be easier than having a face-to-face conversation for some people. You can gain insight on yourself through the eyes of the people who have known you the most. Their perspective can bring to light anything you need to work through as you get into your marriage. As you hand the questions to your parent(s), please be aware that some of their responses may not be as welcoming as you had hoped for them to be. Have an open mind as you read their responses and remember, they are sharing from their perspective. This is also an opportunity to openly communicate their hopes about your marriage to you, hopefully setting the tone for conversations to come.

For the Parent

As a parent, there are insights you have of your child that he or she may not even be aware of. You have also gained a wealth of experience in your married life or your life as a single parent. If your child handed you a printout of these questions for you to fill out, answer them as if your child were facing you and asking you the questions. Where you do not have the answers, it is OK to leave them blank, but please try to respond to all the questions. Please make sure you return the form to your child within a week or less.

1. What are some of the strengths you have seen in me that will help me build a healthy marriage?
2. What three areas of weakness do you see in me that could potentially threaten my marriage?

3. How would you suggest I continue to build on my strengths and work on my weaknesses?
4. As you prepare to welcome a daughter- or son-in-law into your home and life, what would you like for them to know about you?
5. In your experience and observation, what advice would you give me on the following areas?
    - Finances
    - Relating with in-laws
    - Parenting
    - Sex
    - Communication
    - Roles and responsibilities
    - Spiritual growth
6. As we prepare for our wedding day, are there any unresolved issues you would like to discuss with me?
7. What three memories of your marriage have you cherished the most?
8. As we prepare for our marriage, there may be some expected traditions we may choose not to keep as a family. How does this make you feel? Is there any tradition you expect us to keep? If so, please explain your answer.
9. How have some of the hard times you have had in your marriage helped strengthen your faith and also your marriage? Would you share with me at least one of those hard times?
10. What will you cherish the most about raising me, and what will you miss the most as I transition to build my own home?

Sample Wedding Budget

Here is a sample budget to estimate and plan for your wedding. If you still need to make another traditional visit or contribute toward the initial dowry payments, include it in the "other" category. When budgeting for food, plan for an additional 10 per cent of your total invitations to include those who are unlikely to RSVP. Include room and board if you will be catering for relatives travelling from afar.

CASH ON HAND	
From couple	
Family	
Friends	
PROJECTED EXPENSES	
Wedding gown & accessories	
Wedding suit & accessories	
Wedding/reception decor	
Food	
Transport	
Wedding venue	
Reception venue	
Wedding cards	
Honeymoon	
Photographer/videographer	
Other	

HONORARIUM	
MC	
Pastor/Officiant	
Musicians	
Other	
	TOTAL
Balance from cash in hand	

Sample Budget

Here is a sample budget you can use to estimate and plan how you will spend money as a couple each month. Try filling it out together and discussing it.

INCOME PER MONTH	
Salary	
Other	
EXPENSES PER MONTH	
CONTRIBUTIONS	
Tithe	
Tax	
Mandatory contributions	
HOUSING	
Rent/Mortgage	
Electricity	
Water	
Garbage Collection	
Phone	
Maintenance	
Other	
FOOD	
Groceries	

VEHICLE(S)	
Payments	
Insurance	
Fuel	
Maintenance	
INSURANCE	
Medical	
Life	
Other	
DEBTS	
School Loans	
Credit Cards	
Other	
ENTERTAINMENT	
Eating Out	
Vacations	
Activities	
Other	
CLOTHING	
Clothing, shoes, etc.	
SAVINGS/INVESTMENTS	
Bank	
SACCO	
Chama	
Other Investments	

MEDICAL EXPENSES (Not covered by insurance)	
Doctor	
Dentist	
Medicine	
Other	
OTHER HOUSEHOLD NEEDS	
Toiletries	
Beauty/salon/barber	
Drycleaners	
House-help	
Other	
OTHER EXPENSES	
Family Support	
Offering	
Charity	
	TOTAL EXPENSES
INCOME VS. EXPENSES	
Income	
Expenses	
	TOTAL BALANCE

For the Mentor Couple

Are You Ready to Become a Mentor?

It is likely that your parents or grandparents still tell stories of their lives in village communities where they had access to family members who stood as exemplary to them. Whether intending to or not, these people served as their mentors. Compare their lives with yours, and you see how living away from the comfort of a family community and a shift in values has meant less access to natural mentorship opportunities. Young people are now meeting each other in their adopted communities, and they have few to no mentors to guide them in their decisions. They are getting married and moving on to build families on foundations that would be stronger if they had others walk alongside them.

Like never before we need a movement of couples who are willing to guide young people preparing for marriage: to share their stories, to discuss lessons learned in their journey of marriage, to intentionally dive into the Bible and learn together about the institution of marriage. Couples preparing for marriage are aware of their many friends who struggle in their marriages. They do not want to end up like their friends, but they do not know where to go for help. They want to learn how to build intimacy and live out God's purpose and plan for their marriage. And, even when many of them may not tell you this, their ultimate desire is to grow closer to God, whose truth can and will transform their relationship, their family, and those around them.

Would you consider mentoring a young couple as they prepare for their marriage?

You Can Lead as a Mentor Couple

Can you, with your strengths and weaknesses, be used by God to help a couple prepare for their marriage? Absolutely, yes! As children of God who are called to make disciples wherever you go, you have an opportunity to make a difference in couples' lives as you disciple them into a strong foundation for their marriage.

You do not have to have a perfect marriage – no one does! If you have been married for at least five years and are willing to grow your marriage as God guides from his Word, then you are the right person to mentor a couple preparing for marriage.

Frequently Asked Questions

WE DON'T THINK WE HAVE THE TIME.

With countless responsibilities competing for your attention, it makes sense that you, as a couple, feel that you do not have time to be mentors to a couple preparing for marriage. However, the benefits of being mentors can save you time as a couple when you consider that you will be investing time to build your own marriage, you will be studying the Word of God together, you will be growing in intimacy with Christ, you will be having fun, you will be making new friends, and you will also serve God by serving the church.

OUR MARRIAGE IS FAR FROM BEING PERFECT, SO HOW CAN WE MENTOR OTHERS TO BUILD A STRONG MARRIAGE?

You actually could be the best couple to mentor a young couple. If you are willing to share about your successes and weaknesses as you seek God to grow together in your marriage, you become a real, live model to the young couple. They already know there is no perfect marriage. What they need is to hear from a couple who is willing to admit to it and still commit to build their marriage using biblical principles. When the couple see that you are still learning how to build your marriage, they are more prone to warm up to you and trust you than if you presented a perfect picture that they already suspect does not exist.

WE ARE NOT TRAINED TO LEAD COUPLES IN THESE SESSIONS.

This is not a problem at all. Your role is to facilitate, not be an expert. The sessions are presented in a way that you only need to read through the material and discuss it with them. After every session, they have an activity to do before your next session. When you meet for the next session, you will hear feedback from them about the activity and offer clarity where it may be needed.

If it is your first time to lead something like this, here are a few basic facilitation tips. As you guide the discussion, make sure you are staying on the subject. Provide a warm environment. Be accepting of each other and of the couple. That's all! You will do a great job! With your desire to love and encourage the couple and to practice hospitality, you will find the experience rewarding.

WHAT IF THE COUPLE HAVE PROBLEMS THAT WE DO NOT HAVE ANSWERS TO?

Remember, you are not wearing the hat of an expert but one of a couple who is willing to facilitate discussions. Should the couple have challenges that seem to need an expert, feel free to suggest a counsellor or therapist. If you are not sure who that would be, use your church as a place to get more information.

Leading through the Sessions

There are 10 sessions to go through, including the discussion on the **Personal History Data**. The first session can be easily combined with the Personal History Data, and the 10th and 11th sessions can also be combined. You can choose to meet once a week or once every two weeks. Whichever you decide, be sure to have the couple do their homework projects for the preceding session before your next meeting. Before you move on to the next session, have the couple share about the homework. Since your meetings can take anywhere from nine to eighteen weeks, depending which meeting timetable you settle on, be sure to start the sessions at least three months before the couple's wedding.

The sessions are presented to make it easy for you to lead with little preparation. Familiarize yourself with the session, and especially highlight concepts that stand out. One of the best ways to prepare is to pray together as a couple, asking God to prepare your and the couple's hearts, to guide each one of you, and to teach you by the power of his Holy Spirit.

Keep the discipline of starting and finishing at the agreed-upon times. A session should take an hour, and because you might choose to offer light snacks, give the entire session one and a half hours. If the couple come late, talk about the importance of respecting time, and be sure to model that by being ready every time they arrive.

Before you close a session, pray together with the couple. If you do not know the couple well, model by praying during the first few sessions before you also encourage them to pray. As you send them away, remind them of any homework or discussions they might need to work through before your next meeting. Make sure you all put on your calendar the next date and time you have agreed to meet. If the couple have a discussion they need to work through before the next session, ask them to also agree on a date and put it in their diary before they leave your meeting.

Between sessions, send the couple a reminder about their discussion questions and about your next meeting. Remind them you are thinking of them and ask them to think through one or two take-aways from your last session. Keeping that line of communication open shows that you care and are glad you are walking with them.

Presenting the Gospel

We hope and pray you will be approached by couples who are believers and those who are not believers. As the non-believing couple begin to see the practical application of the Bible in marriage, opportunities to further discuss spirituality will present themselves. As a mentor couple, we hope you will take up the opportunity to share with them the need for a personal relationship with Jesus. You can share about your life before you came to faith, how you made the decision, and what difference your decision has made in your life and specifically your marriage. While you cannot twist their arms and coerce them into salvation, you have a platform to plant a seed and leave it to God to water it.

When All Is Said and Done

Your commitment to meet with this couple is for a limited amount of time. However, as the couple moves into their marriage, leave the door open for them to reach out to you with any questions. If you know of a study for couples desiring to build their marriages, tell them about it. We have included suggestions in **Further Resources** on the next page. Encourage them to seek out other couples to grow with once they are married. Just as it is important for you to continue building your marriage, it is also important for them to do the same.

Further Resources

Books

Love & Respect: The Love She Most Desires; The Respect He Desperately Needs by Dr Emerson Eggerichs

Intended for Pleasure: Sex Technique and Sexual Fulfillment in Christian Marriage by Ed Wheat, M.D., and Gaye Wheat

The Act of Marriage: Christian Guide to Sexual Love by Tim F. LaHaye and Beverly LaHaye

Staying Close: Stopping the Natural Drift Toward Isolation in Marriage by Dennis Rainey

Sheet Music: Uncovering the Secrets of Sexual Intimacy in Marriage by Dr Kevin Leman

Sexual Intimacy in Marriage by William Cutrer and Sandra Glahn

Couples Studies

HomeBuilders Couples Series (FamilyLife)

The Art of Marriage (LifeWay – FamilyLife)

Articles

www.thrivingmarriages.com

www.familylife.com

Equip Your Premarital Ministry

There are many resources which can equip your premarital ministry, including some which have been created in Africa. Oasis recommends:

BAESICS: RUN HARD AFTER GOD, IF ANYONE CATCHES UP, INTRODUCE YOURSELF

Ernest Wamboye with Waturi Wamboye

In *Baesics*, Ernest and Waturi Wamboye give no-nonsense advice on how to build a fulfilling love life and marriage. Young adults in African cities feel marriage is priority but are often unprepared. *Baesics* addresses the relationship dilemmas many young adults are facing today from a Christian point of view.

Baesics urges you to:

- Commit yourself wholeheartedly to Christ.
- Find your identity and purpose before you find a partner.
- Set appropriate sexual and emotional boundaries.

This book addresses the world's myths about what makes one a man or a woman, how to handle temptations such as lust, and how to deal with emotional wounds. Learn the basics for choosing your bae so you can lay a biblical foundation for your love life and the marriage you desire.

A PRE-MARRIAGE COUNSELLING HANDBOOK: FOR PASTORS AND LAY COUNSELLORS

Alan & Donna Goerz

A Pre-Marriage Counselling Handbook was written specifically for the African context on how to build a successful marriage. Covering topics such as:

- Getting to know your spouse
- Communication skills and conflict resolution
- Marriage vows
- What the Bible says about sex
- In-law relationships
- Financial home management
- Preparing a godly home for children
- Building a biblical foundation

Designed as a seminar-in-a-book, *A Pre-Marriage Counselling Handbook* equips pastors and counselors to teach biblical pre-marriage classes and seminars.

THE SISTERHOOD SECRET: CHANGING THE WORLD TOGETHER, ONE WOMAN AT A TIME

Levina Mulandi

The Sisterhood Secret expounds on Titus 2 to give women an in-depth guide on how to disciple younger women in all areas of life. In *The Sisterhood Secret*, Dr Levina Mulandi casts a vision by telling stories of some of the 50 women in Nairobi, Kenya she has discipled.

More than Bible study or a church program, Dr Mulandi shares how she empowers any woman to mentor younger women, guiding them to understand their identity, discern the purpose of their lives, and be transformed to be more like Christ. The women that Dr Mulandi has walked with have mentored dozens more through this life-on-life discipleship model which is a family relationship between sisters in Christ.

oasisinternationalpublishing.com | oasisinternational.com